Queen City Yesterdays

Queen City Yesterdays

SKETCHES OF CINCINNATI IN THE 1880s

WILLIAM C. SMITH

WITH AN INTRODUCTION AND NOTES
BY HIS LONG-TIME FRIEND FLAXIUS

Commonwealth Book Company
St. Martin, Ohio

Copyright © 1959 by William C. Smith
Originally published in a limited edition of 1000 copies
Copyright © 2023 by Commonwealth Book Company

All rights reserved. No part of this book may be reproduced in any form
or by any means without the prior written consent of the
publisher, excepting brief quotes used in reviews.
Printed in the United States of America.

ISBN: 978-1-948986-65-6

THE AUTHOR

William C. Smith must be a sore disappointment to detective story addicts who picture an antiquarian bookseller as a dusty cadaver in black alpaca and a skullcap. At eighty-seven Smith is a dapper, rotund gentleman, invariably in immaculate linen. No skullcap graces his pink and white brow and he is a solid hundred pounds too heavy to compete in the cadaver class.

Born and reared in Cincinnati, Smith has all of what have long been recognized as the Cincinnati virtues—competence in business and a love of good food, drink, conversation, and books. He became a discriminating and voracious reader when, as he says, "they let me learn to read in the first grade." In maturity his favorite fare has been folkways, anthropology and the language and literature of the Gypsy.

In 1898 Smith opened his first book store. Locating on Fourth Street, he carried fine editions and remainders. He closed this out in the feverish days of World War I but in 1918 he established the Smith Book Company with offices in the Union Central Building. There he specialized in Americana and developed a trade that extended throughout the world.

In 1955 Smith decided to retire. He reminded his friends that he would soon be eighty-four, that commuting from his home in Fort Thomas, Kentucky, was a nuisance, that overhead was scandalous and that, as his catalog had reminded the public for years, "Rare books are getting scarce." Besides, he had worked long enough: "I could say I am going to raise dahlias and commune with Nature," he wrote, "but it would be an untruth. I never cared much for Nature."

Smith gave up his lease, sold his stock and retired. But he continued to come into the city a couple of times a week to lunch with young book-trade cronies. Inevitably he encountered an occasional book that looked like a bargain. Old suppliers, not aware of his new status, continued to offer items and elderly Cincinnatians still called him when the time came to settle the family estate. Within a few months Smith was back in the business, issuing catalogs and buying and selling as avidly as ever, his study at home serving as office.

He is still at it and likely to continue for a long, long time. His favorite grandfather was still hale and in business when he caught cold and pneumonia took him at seventy-eight: the grandson has never had a cold in his life. —FLAXIUS

A Note

In 1880, the census year in which the author must have first become cognizant of his surroundings in the Queen City (even then still called "Porkopolis" by neighbors jealous of its prosperous packing industry) Cincinnati was a western metropolis of 255,000 souls.

The place had been in existence a trifle under a century—pretty long by Midwestern standards of the day—having been originally conceived in 1788 by Matthias Denman and Robert Patterson with the unfortunate John Filson as a third. Poor Filson did a little surveying, probably helped dream up the original name of the town, and was murdered not far from its limits by persons presumed to be Indians. That original name, "Losantiville" simply must have originated in the fey mind of Filson; it was explained as deriving "*L* for Licking [River], *os* for mouth, *anti* for opposite and *ville* for town" —("town opposite the mouth of the Licking River" that would be, friend, in case you haven't already caught on!)

That conception had the virtue of originality, but it lasted only until some former officers of the Revolutionary forces, having formed themselves into The Society of the Cincinnati in 1783, moved west to the new town and suggested that its name be changed to honor their organization. It was.

The place was fortunate from its beginning. It attracted these officers, most of whom were literate men still young and several cuts in culture above the mill-run of western emigrants of the day. Other early residents were some of the more enterprising of the Scotch-Irish traders originally settled around Fort Pitt, and men direct from the Atlantic seaboard who had capital to invest and saw the town as the key to a great trading area.

Possibly the most distinctive mark put on the community as it matured was that of the German emigration that began in the period 1820-1830 and was much augmented in 1848, when political upheavals drove many intellectuals from Germany. Their choice, at home, was to emigrate or hang, but many of them were of the cream of their native land. Prosperity—with a growing interest in music, literature, and good eating and drinking—marked any city in which these "achtafurtziger" ("forty-eighters") settled. While many of them moved on west to Louisville and St. Louis, the majority chose to stay in Cincinnati: enough, indeed, to make "Tzinzinnati," pronounced with what was believed to be a German accent, a popular catchword among stage comedians for decades to come.

The Cincinnati of William C. Smith's first memory (he was born on January 23rd, 1872) was a prosperous city. His fellow-citizens were people who could look back on a long American background, or toward a fairly recent Continental origin. Cincinnati had a more cosmopolitan outlook, bought and read more books, enjoyed better food, supported more theatre seats per capita, owned more public parks—and, one supposes, had more fun, wholesome and otherwise —than any city in the United States excepting possibly San Francisco. Cincinnati was an excellent background for Smith—and Smith a suitable ornament for Cincinnati.

—FLAXIUS

Mr. Smith's essays begin with a description of the West End, his own boyhood stamping-ground. As a resident of the corner of Seventh and Central he naturally selects Central Avenue, mainstem of that neighborhood, for his attention.

1
Central Avenue

Central Avenue, or "Western Row" as the older people of that time still called it, was the main artery leading to the West End. From Fifth Street to Mohawk, a distance of about one mile, nearly the entire length of the street was given over to various business enterprises. Most of the shops were small one-man affairs operated by the owner, with perhaps one assistant; saloons were the exception, for the aristocratic dispensers of the amber fluid, in addition to the proprietor, required the services of a bartender, a porter, and a cook for free lunch.

Recollection falters in any attempt to picture the various types of business located in any one mile of this shopping center. A furniture store at Fifth and Central Avenue got the parade off to a good start and was followed by pawn shops, a book store, groceries, barber shops, shoe stores, dry goods stores, cigar stores, and a host of others, plentifully seasoned with saloons.

Barber shops of the better class provided another service in addition to their regular vocation of shaving and haircutting. These shops displayed signs in the window reading "Baths Twenty-five Cents." The regular price for shaving was fifteen cents; for hair cutting, twenty-five cents; and tips were unknown. One shop, operated by two of our colored brethren and located at George and Plum Streets, had a sign in the window, "Shaves five cents, hair cutting ten cents."

Dry goods stores were well represented on the Avenue. Ready-to-wear garments for women were practically unknown; piece goods, ranging from calico and gingham to wool and silk, were sold by the yard. Such yardage, along with the necessary trimmings, linings, etc., were purchased and turned over to a professional dressmaker who constructed the finished horror then in style. Dresses were worn full length and flared out at the bottom end of the skirt, thus consuming enough yardage to make a fair sized tent. Flounces, gatherings, and other furbelows were scattered over the area in great confusion. The building of a fancy dress of the period necessitated employing a dressmaker with the training of an architect. The more opulent families employed, once or twice a year, a resident dressmaker who lived with the family for a period long enough to create whatever garments were required and also such items as sheets, pillow-cases, shams, and a pair of jeans pants for the young of the male species. The construction of a silk dress, quite a luxury, called for a cabinet meeting which was in session for several months debating the kind of material, style, etc. Relatives and friends were called on for advice and the enterprise was kicked around a long time before they arrived at a decision and began to break ground.

Indians were plentiful on the Avenue but they were of the inanimate type, constructed of wood, and stood on pedestals in front of cigar stores. The tobacco industry was well represented as, in addition to the regular dealers, cigars, cigarettes, and chewing tobacco were stocked by some groceries. None of the higher priced or imported brands of cigars were offered by the cigar stores in the West End. Cigar prices ranged from two for five cents to ten cents each. Chewing tobacco came packed in wooden containers, each holding a dozen or more one-pound plugs. A slicing machine for cutting pound plugs into five and ten cent cuts was in evidence on the counter. Star, Horseshoe, Gravely, and Splendid were popular brands of chewing tobacco; scrap, the left-over cuttings in the manufacture of cigars, was favored by those addicts of the weed who preferred the straight article without sweetening or flavor; this was sold in plain paper bags at five cents. Fine cut, another type of chewing tobacco, was shredded, sweetened, and flavored and was packaged in a large wooden bucket and sold by the ounce. Twist, just plain tobacco in a twisted roll, was used for both chewing and smoking. Snuff was housed in a stone jar and was doled out by the ounce. Not over half a dozen kinds of cigarettes were stocked; Old Judge, Richmond Straight Cut, and Sweet Caporal were popular brands. Pipe tobacco in a dozen varieties was packed in cloth sacks, cardboard, and tin.

There were two drug stores located on opposite corners of Sixth Street and Central Avenue, each of them staffed by the proprietor, a clerk and a utility boy. Soda water, with nectar the popular flavor, was dispensed at five cents the glass; later, when a dollop of ice cream was added, the price was advanced to ten cents. Prescriptions averaged around seventy-five cents. The mainstay of the drug stores was the large number of patent medicines, lotions, salves, physics, and ointments with which their shelves were loaded. The wild claims made for the curative power of these concoctions would make interesting reading to-day: if one could credit their claims, there could be no illness and death itself would be postponed indefinitely. None of them, however, claimed to bring back the dead—this chore was monopolized by certain saloons who specialized in a drink known as a "corpse reviver."

Shoes were sold at prices ranging from one and one half to three dollars; the cheaper variety were pegged, that is, the soles were attached to the uppers with small wooden pegs; the better class were sewed. Boots were usually worn in winter and were especially popular with younger generation males. Shoes were the old style high variety, either laced or buttoned. Laced shoes presented no problem to anyone with a high instep as the adjustment was simple; buttoned shoes required alteration; the buttons were removed and a machine operated by foot power provided the necessary slack. Another type of shoe called the "Congress" consisted of a sole and an upper built high enough to cover the ankle. Inserted in the sides of the uppers were pieces of elastic cloth. This shoe could be pulled on like a boot and was in favor with the more indolent type of the male animal.

Candy stores of the better class stocked mixed candies such as are on sale to-day but the variety was limited. The cheaper type of neighborhood candy shops could be found in most localities and always in such strategic locations as the vicinity of a school-house. They were more primitive; their stock consisted of licorice drops, gum drops, stick candy such as mint and horehound, cocoanut bars, a combination of cocoanuts and molasses, all-day suckers, jaw-breakers, and pan candy, cream, chocolate, and molasses. These pan candies came in tin pans about two feet square, a chunk would be pried out, placed in the palm of one hand and cracked with a small hammer; the segments were then weighed and wrapped in newspaper. There was nothing objectionable about this process as far as either merchant or customer was concerned: everyone's hands were considered clean unless proved otherwise.

Pawn shops and other dealers in second-hand clothing required the services of a bushelman: this breed of tailor was hired to re-vamp and repair men's clothing so that it could be worked off on the night trade under a flickering gas jet where it was difficult to detect crude repairs. Dry cleaning was in its infancy and the bushelman's method of removing grease spots was to iron them out or cover them with something that blended with the rest of the landscape. On black garments, ink was a favorite. Pants were usually lined with a light cotton material which was renewed in the second-hand article, giving the garments a new lease on life.

Clothing stores, dealing in ready-made garments for men, kept their stock piled on counters, a dozen or more coats, pants and vests in separate piles. The try-on was rudimentary; alterations, if any, were made at the expense of the buyer who enlisted the services of a bushelman for the purpose. Usually if the trousers were too long, a couple of hitches with the suspenders, or "galluses" as they were termed, made the necessary adjustment. If the waist line soared half-way to the chin this was a mere detail. Pants pockets opened at the top of the trousers instead of the sides, making it quite a strain on the elbow to dive into such high-waisted articles. Manufacturers of ready-made clothing provided a standard pattern and it was up to the buyer to adjust his anatomy to conform to their ground plans.

In place of the modern garage, livery stables were found in most middle class localities. Only the wealthy could afford a carriage and horses: an outfit comprising two nags, a carriage, and harness ran close to a two thousand dollar investment and also called for a coachman and stable. The more impecunious, when it became necessary to "put on the dog," resorted to the livery stable which would, for a price, supply the entire show: horses, carriage, a man in livery, and perhaps even a coach dog under the rig for the more demanding. To-day, a flossy layout would require a dog license, a driver's license, rent-a-car hire—and even so the customer would have to provide his own livery and do the driving.

The author's somewhat irreverent boyhood attitude toward them notwithstanding, the Cincinnati Public Schools did very well by him. As he has been quoted elsewhere, "they let him learn to read"—and appear to have encouraged him to continue to do so, widely and in many fields. He received a grounding in mathematics that is seldom known to-day except by the dedicated. He learned to write the sort of copper-plate hand now admired by all, practiced by few under fifty and looked upon with horror by Dewey's followers. He learned some history and geography and acquired a thirst for further information on these subjects that has directed his reading every since.

Naturally his free spirit resisted some of the formalities of education practiced in his day:

2
School Days

The first school I attended was the Eighth District, located on Eighth Street near John. I put in one year there before someone discovered I resided on the *East* side of Central Avenue, which was in the Ninth District, Central Avenue being the dividing line. The Ninth District School was located on Ninth Street near Race about five blocks distant. After serving my time there the next step was the Second Intermediate School at Ninth and Main Streets, about eight blocks from home, and that period was followed by one at Woodward High School. Woodward called for a trek of one and one half miles.

School sessions were from nine to twelve in the morning and from one-thirty to four in the afternoon, relieved by a fifteen minute recess in each session. The interval between twelve and one-thirty gave ample time to make the round trip home and back, with time to spare to put on the nose bag.

The Intermediate School premises were limited to an area that left no room for anything in the way of games—just standing room, where the boys could gather in groups, gnaw on a pretzel and discuss the sins of their ancestors, their school teachers, and other objectionable specimens of the human race. The school-house, still standing as I write, is a structure of three floors with the interior dividing walls constructed of brick, which, with iron stairways, constituted a primitive attempt to make the edifice fire-proof. The floors were wood and the heating was provided by a monster of a stove in each room. These stoves consisted of a large casing of iron in which was placed a fire-box of some vitrified material, leaving an empty space between the fire-box and the outer casing. Each had a damper arrangement covering the entire top, which could be, and was, opened or closed from time to time for some reasons mysterious to all but teachers and janitor as there was no direct connection with the fire. This school boasted a janitor whose duties were to sweep the rooms and halls in the morning and, in winter, to build a fire in each room. The result of this schedule was that the rooms were seldom comfortable until noon.

It happened one day, on the occasion of some horse-play on the part of a number of boys who were in the room before class time, that a plug of tobacco, either by accident or design, was dropped into the space between the fire-box and the outer iron casing of the stove. Class opened before the foreign substance could be retrieved. For about one hour peace and quite reigned, then a small wisp of smoke made its appearance at the top of the machine (or utensil) and increased in volume until it became a close relative of the fogs that plague the city of London. This smoke carried an aroma quite pleasing to those of the tribe known as "chew tobacco loafers" but it had devastating effect on such pure-souled youths, male and female, as were not addicted to the weed or aware of its properties. Opening the windows was no remedy; this pall of gloom had found a good place to light and decided to stay. The janitor was summoned and with the aid of a pair of tongs, removed the smouldering plug and hove it out of the window.

A number of boys at Intermediate either chewed tobacco or smoked. The smokers had no remedy but those who chewed, while they could not practice their pet vice fully in class, could take a small piece of the weed and let it lie dormant in the mouth to kill their craving until recess or after school, when they could do the job according to Hoyle.

One genius, who was never discovered, evolved a system whereby he could get the full benefit of the chewing process while being educated: each desk had in one corner a small well in which was deposited a bottle of ink. This resourceful criminal was wont to empty his ink bottle, utilize it as a gaboon and then, as opportunity offered, trade ink bottles with some innocent youth who was not addicted to the weed.

{One suspects the culprit's name may possibly have begun with "S."—FLAXIUS, *ed.}*

Our teacher of arithmetic, "Daddy Orr," had the chewing habit himself and at times indulged during class. He could hold the juice for some time, but at the end of the limit of his retentive power he would then casually walk to the door, stick his head out into the hall and shoot the contents down the stairs. This habit resulted in a happy accident that made student life worth living for a considerable period.

On that occasion Daddy fired a stream of the golden fluid down the stairs just as the Principal rounded the corner on the landing halfway below. How much the Principal actually received in the way of decoration we pupils never knew but that we enjoyed the episode is an understatement. As we were all fond of "Daddy Orr" and had no time for the Principal, we felt that Providence was on the job and that justice had been done.

Woodward High School had no intermission long enough to enable us to go home for lunch; the session lasted from nine o'clock in the morning until two-thirty in the afternoon, with a recess of twenty minutes between eleven and twelve. Some of the boys brought a lunch but the majority waited until the session was over and had a belated lunch at home. Being blessed with a voracious appetite, this did not suit my book. I had two chums afflicted with the same craving and we devised a scheme whereby we could procure a hot lunch. There was a saloon a short distance from the school where one could guzzle a glass of beer for five cents and snare a hot dog for the same price, to say nothing of the free lunch. This place was of course out of bounds and a monitor was stationed at the gate to keep the peace and report deserters. The three of us ganged up on this monitor and had a little conversation with him. We intimated that if he overlooked certain of our activities he would, in time, achieve manhood and perhaps be a credit to his parents. This little sermon evidently appealed to him as we were never annoyed by being called before old Harper for a wigging.

High school was just four years of misery, leavened by the fact that I had access to a few books that afforded a much-needed relief. I took little interest in what was dished out in the name of education. How I got through without being cast into outer darkness is a mystery, as I utilized my study hours in reading such books as I found of interest in the miserable collection the school called a library. Any education I acquired during these four years should be credited to Tyler's *Primitive Culture,* Draper's *Intellectual Development of Europe,* a couple of odd volumes of Huxley, Gibbon's *Roman Empire* and Anthon's *Classical Dictionary.* I soon realized what a vast difference there was between the pabulum called history as dished out in the schools and the unadulterated record as presented by Gibbon, etc.

In the Intermediate School, the art of writing was taught by a special teacher who once a week devoted one half hour to that important subject. At the time I wrote a good clear hand, having developed the arm movement and could write for hours without getting writer's cramp. Then some pedagogue stuck his head above the horizon and came up with a new system which the teachers were compelled to enforce. We were made to hold the pen between the thumb and the first two fingers, rest the other fingers on the paper and wiggle the fingers holding the pen. With the teacher standing over us holding a rattan, any deviation from the new system was promptly subdued. Teachers lead an unhappy life and unfortunately they are compelled to transmit their unhappiness and the incompetence of the educationists to their pupils. The educationists in their God-like majesty devise some idiotic system and lay the burden of making it work on the teachers. If it doesn't work, they can always dig up a new one. An educationist delivers to a class of fifty pupils, fifty pairs of shoes all one kind and size. This involves two possible operations; the teacher has to adjust the shoes to the feet or the pupils have to adapt their feet to the shoes.

In those good old days fifty per cent of the pupils in our public schools left school after passing the fourth grade, leaving but half the number for the intermediate schools, fifth to seventh grades, and not more than one-third of the intermediate pupils entered high school. The average I.Q. at that time was the same as it is now, a mentality of from twelve to thirteen years. We got rid of half of the school population after they passed the fourth grade; they got jobs of sorts and later on learned a trade and there was no juvenile delinquency. Now God should take notice, we not only filter them through high school but load them onto the higher institutions of learning, with the result that they come out with a poll parrot memory and an assortment of facts they have memorized without imbibing a single principle. Ninety per cent of the students of to-day are being loaded with information they are not competent to utilize. Any attempt to crowd a quart of liquid into a pint bottle is a sinful waste of good whiskey.

I chose German for one of the courses in High School for the reason that I had a good practical knowledge of it and could get by with a modicum of labor and also invest the time gained in some subject not on the high school menu. Algebra and Geometry were easy and I exchanged my skill in these subjects with another pupil who did my Latin which to me was a nightmare, since the infernal junk was loaded with grammar, my pet aversion. During my last year in intermediate school some fat-headed school administrator had a brain storm and gave birth to an idea that revolutionized the entire system of grading. The daily record for the year was made the basis for promotion, yearly exams being eliminated. Inasmuch as I was one of three rebels who were not permitted to recite in the grammar class, I was handicapped as my daily record was nil. The grammar teacher, a sour old specimen with grammar in her veins instead of blood, tried to keep me out of high school but as my average was well in the eighties, including her goose egg, the Principal turned her down. Whether she wanted me in her class another year for a horrible example or just an ornament is a moot question.

High school sessions allowed an extra hour in the afternoon that could be gainfully employed by rooting through the Cincinnati Public Library, which provided material not available in the school library. I could get what books I wanted from the public library, take them home and keep them a week. Much more satisfying, that was, than the scraps I could get out of the school library during study hours. True, I did swipe some of the books in the school library: I kept them several weeks and they were never missed. Among the treasures discovered in the public library were two little volumes by Edgar Saltus: *The Anatomy of Negation* and *The Philosophy of Disenchantment*. They are still on my "must" list for reading once a year. Spencer's *Philosophy* intrigued me; I couldn't digest it until many years later but conceived an admiration for his careful use of English; he had the knack of saying quite a few things without committing himself to the point where, for even hinting at certain theories fifty years before, he would have been jailed.

High school literature was another bore. When Albert J. Nock was requested to teach a class in English he said "I wouldn't know how to go about it; all I could do would be to refer them to the library and have them help themselves." Brillat Savarin was the king of epicures when it came to putting on the nose bag or sticking both feet in the trough but I cannot see him specifying what I should eat or drink; and that goes for literature.

Our teacher in the sixth grade was the only rebel I ever sat under. He paid no attention to the routine devised by the God-like Authorities; he simply explained the matter in hand, said "study, boys" and left us to our own devices. The result was that about fifteen per cent of the pupils were promoted on their averages; the balance of the class flunked and had to be "put up"—which was the term used for advancing a pupil without benefit of clergy. That was the most profitable of all my school years. Old Woollard put us on our own and made us think. While this system had no value for the majority it was duck soup for the minority who could take it in stride.

It's no great wonder that the present-day school brat is unable to read, write, or figure and thinks Kokomo, Indiana, is a new way to cook sauerkraut. The poor little chap of to-day, is overloaded with extra-curricular activities to such an extent he just has not the time for study, although he glories in luxuries that were not even dreamed of in the old days. It has been said that comparisons have a bad odor but let's take a look at the present picture. The pupil of to-day rides to school, has ample playgrounds, a stadium, a lunch room, a gymnasium, central heating, a large library, and sanitary plumbing. At home he has radio, television, and a telephone. We walked to school. The floors were wooden and dusted daily so that the floating debris settled on our desks; the rooms were seldom comfortably warm before noon; our toilet was the old fashioned out-door variety; if we needed a drink, we sucked it out of a hydrant in the back schoolyard, without benefit of tin cup; if we misbehaved we had our hides lubricated with a dose of rattan—but we could read, write, and figure when we got through.

Try our modern pupils on a simple arithmetic problem, say the insurance rate $21.60 per thousand on $4280.00, and not one in ten will come within three light years of getting the correct answer.

There was time left over after school for play: something like six hours between the closing bell and bedtime. Cincinnati being a city, with lighted streets, some of the best of the play time was that after dark.

The literature of that pseudo-science called "folklore" is cluttered with descriptions of the amusements of the young of Lower Slobbovia and the Kingdom of Mu: Mr. Smith tells us of those popular in Cincinnati, Ohio, within historic times.

3
Games

Playgrounds of the modern type were an unknown quantity, as I have said; our amusements were conducted under the most primitive conditions and according to our rules.

The boys' section of the school yard of the Second Intermediate School on Ninth Street had a side yard not over twelve feet wide that ran the length of the building, then widened to about thirty feet, part of which was occupied by an outhouse; the girls' yard on the other side of the building was of like proportions and area. In the rear of each yard was a hydrant and when we needed a drink we sucked it out of the stream, fresh from the nozzle.

Games such as "Hunt the Hare," "Prisoners' Base" and "Vineyard" were played in the streets or alleys. The various games of marbles, the Fat, the Long, and the Bull Ring, were played on the sidewalks. "Follow-up" was better adapted to the street which was sufficiently endowed with mud to lend itself to the technique of this particular pastime.

A simple type of baseball was played in alleys with a soft ball and a barrel stave for a bat; it could not be played in the street owing to the interference of traffic. When we had time on Saturdays or holidays to put on a more elaborate show, the nearest field available was about two miles away in the West End bottoms. As we seldom had sufficient players to staff two nines, we resorted to the type of baseball known as "Scrub." This game required thirteen players, four batters and the usual nine in the field; we did our own umpiring. When a batter was put out, he was banished to right field where he could work his way through each position until he was again eligible as batter. A good ball cost one dollar and it was a rare and gala occasion when we were able to indulge in such luxury: cheaper balls rated from ten to twenty cents and were usually worn out before the end of the game.

The Buchholtz Livery Stable on Seventh Street had the care of more wagons than it could house in its limited quarters and the overflow was parked for the night on the South side of Seventh Street. These rows of vehicles were made to order for the game "I Spy." Some special types with a high seat served a nobler purpose; they were dragged to a lamp post, and the seat about level with the light afforded opportunity for reading dime novels and other contraband literature.

Tick Tack, a relatively harmless annoyance to organized society, required a long black thread, say around seventy-five feet or at least long enough for the operator to locate some place to hide. The thread was attached to the window frame with a pin or a tack and had a small piece of lead or some metal fastened on the thread about ten inches lower. The operator could pull the thread a short way and let it fall back against the window pane. When this aroused the inmates of the house they would try to locate the noise and in doing so raised the window—but the device could not be detected as it went up with the window. When a householder tumbled to the racket, it was a simple matter to give a hard jerk on the thread and walk away with the evidence for use elsewhere. Black thread had still another role; stretched at a calculated height from a post at the curb to the wall of a house it was a menace to such then popular and highly eligible head-gear as plug hats or square-crowned derbies.

Sling shots, the commercial kind with an iron prong, could be had for ten cents but were only bought by the filthy rich: two pennies would buy the required rubber, a small piece of leather could be had for nothing at a cobbler shop and a prong of wood was available for the labor involved in cutting and trimming—a certain churchyard in our neighborhood afforded a plentiful supply. For ammunition, a small round pellet of lead was best for both accuracy and range—not that there was really ever much in the shape of accuracy but it pleased us to think so and brag about it. As lead was not commonly for sale in small lots, we resorted to another church nearby for a supply. This particular church had a wall in which, at intervals, stretches of an iron grill were let into the stone coping and lead poured around the iron to anchor it. A chisel and a little energy was sufficient equipment to enable any ambitious boy to secure a supply, while an iron pot, a fire in the alley, and a bullet mold provided the finished product.

Roller skating in summer and ice skating in winter were popular amusements with the Seventh Street crowd—but the George Street gang, of a lower income with one or two exceptions, were unable to acquire skates owing to the high price of the article which ran into three figures, two of the figures being pennies. Roller skating on Seventh Street was limited to the block between Plum and Elm Streets, where the sidewalks were constructed of flagstone. Other blocks were nearly all paved with brick interspersed with an occasional stretch of stone walk and one superlatively elegant stretch of fancy cement blocks, the only one of its kind on Seventh Street. Brick sidewalks were not adapted to roller skating: they were hard on skates and could be equally hard on the skater.

A pond in Lincoln Park was a favorite place for ice skating but was usually so crowded that any fancy movements were impossible. The old canal, only five blocks distant, was far better; on its stretches there was no room for fancy figures but for straightaway skating it was ideal—and for fancy operation we could always skate out to the first or second basin, an enlargement of the canal several miles north where canal boats were reversed for the return trip. At the basins we, figuratively speaking, sometimes ran into a "burned bridge" as the slaughter houses and breweries in the North end of the town utilized the canal for their supply of ice. Occasionally we encountered open water where ice had been cut and this involved a portage of ten or twelve blocks.

A number of Seventh Street boys owned velocipedes but had but little joy in their operation as there was only one block in the vicinity where such vehicles could be used without jolting loose the soul-case of the rider. Some older boys had bicycles, the old high wheel kind, a large high wheel in front with a small wheel behind. To ride these, one foot had to be placed on a small step attached to the spine while the other hind leg provided the motive power. When sufficient speed was attained, the rider made a wild leap for the saddle and began pawing for the pedals. If he landed in time and had a lucky break with the pedals he could get along: if not, he usually landed on his face in the street while the spine and the little hind wheel soared aloft. Any small obstruction struck by the large front wheel while in motion would bring on a similar disaster.

Race Street was the first street in Cincinnati to be paved with asphalt; Seventh Street was so treated a year or so later. Seventh Street had a street car track in its middle, while Race Street had none: as a result Race Street became a cyclist's heaven. Each bicycle was equipped with a bell attached to the handle bar, which served as a warning to pedestrians, and swinging from the hub, inside the big wheel, was a lantern—an additional notice to jay-walkers to jump or die. Speeding was a word not in use as applied to these menaces; the term in vogue was "scorching."

The entire wheel except the saddle was nickel-plated, which entailed an amount of labor with one or another sorts of ointment to keep the contraption in its original state of glittering elegance. In time, keeping the machine clean and polished, and riding the thing, became a fifty-fifty proposition: half use, half maintenance. This is to be interpreted literally—not in the sense of that one-horse, one-rabbit, French recipe for rabbit pie.

The game "Cat" was popular with the small fry and was played on the streets or on the sidewalks. A small piece of wood some seven or eight inches in length with a diameter of one and one half inches was whittled to a point at each end. One end was struck with a stick and as it rose in the air several feet the operator was supposed to use his stick as a bat and drive it some distance, after which the performance was repeated. The other players surrounded the batter and endeavored to catch the cat before it landed, in which event the batter was retired and the lucky catcher had his turn at bat. A somewhat similar game played by the larger boys was "Boulder off." A flat stone was used as a base and on it was placed a boulder. One boy stood guard over the base and the other players, each armed with another boulder in hand took turns in taking a shot at the boulder on the base. The play was to knock off the boulder and recover one's own missile before the guard could replace the boulder on the stone. If the thrower made the grade he would tag his opponent, who then took his place as guard.

Rain was drained off the roofs of the German-style houses by way of a tin tube terminating in an iron contraption at the lower end called a downspout. Water from this source was discharged on the sidewalk where it wended its way to the gutter: water used by householders for various purposes followed the same trail. This ready access to water provided a form of amusement that is not available to youngsters to-day. Syringes consisting of a small tube of wood into which was inserted a plunger with a string wrapped around the end to insure suction were on sale at five cents each: the ammunition provided by the gutters cost nothing and the use of this weapon can be left to the imagination. Not being millionaires, able to throw five-cent pieces around indiscriminately, my particular chum and I conceived a measure whereby we could compete with this monopoly, provide ourselves with weapons, and rake in a considerable profit on the side.

This inspiration was not derived from some unadulterated society of saints but more likely came from a region far removed from the saintly habitat. We purchased a bamboo fishing pole for ten cents, cut it into sections, carved out a wooden plunger with the aid of a saw and a drawknife and, behold! we had a home-made article with twice the capacity and three times the range of the commercial type. These articles we retailed to the gang for ten cents for the sections at the butt of the pole and five cents for those of lesser capacity, at the upper end.

Aside from our venture in the manufacture of syringes, my chum (Frank Smith, no immediate relation but one of the royal family) and I engaged in another enterprise that produced once a year a plushy income. Parades, consisting of elaborate "floats," as they were called, displaying allegories and historic characters and events, were yearly affairs. Such parades always passed Seventh and Central Avenue and attracted crowds that were nearly solid back on the sidewalks, from curb to wall. Several weeks in advance of these affairs, Frank and I gathered all the wooden boxes of various sizes that we could procure in the neighborhood and stored them in our back yards. On parade nights, we would peddle these boxes at from ten to twenty-five cents each, usually to some chap accompanied by an undersized female, who would then chivalrously mount her on the box and provide her with an unobstructed view of the spectacle. This enterprise netted from five to seven dollars each year and for some time after our Dun and Bradstreet rating was "A-1:" I could not estimate how many romances we inadvertently promoted, nor, I am happy to say, how they turned out. I shall not describe our method of procuring the boxes. The word "procure" is a conveniently flexible term that can cover a multitude of sins.

Still another item of commerce could be listed under the "procure" category. Most any boy had a wagon of sorts, either the commercial variety which could be had for a couple of dollars or the better and sturdier type that were home-made. The only outlay of cash necessary was ten cents for the purchase of four solid wooden wheels from a factory on Plum Street, the balance of the material was acquired by the "procure" method. A board about six feet in length and sixteen inches wide formed the bed of the wagon. Such boards were acquired in devious ways; if at times a householder found a board missing in his back fence, he would usually attribute his loss to the act of some vandal in need of kindling wood and as old boards had no earmarks, we got away with the loot. Attached to the board were two axles carved out of a chunk of wood, with a saw and drawknife. A bolt was inserted in the front end of the bed-board, running through the front axle and a notch was cut in each side of the board at the proper place insuring a short turn. The hole for the bolt, in the absence of an augur of suitable size, could be bored with a hot poker. Bolts, cotter pins for the wheels and other trifles utilized in the making presented no difficulties as they too could be "procured."

Another type of vehicle, more of a cart than a wagon and with less carrying capacity, was made from a soap box. The two hind wheels of an abandoned velocipede were used, the iron axle was laid into a wooden base which had a groove carved out with a chisel, the axle being held in place by staples. While designed for light loads, they were sturdy enough to haul home such heavy commodities as a five gallon coal oil can. Soap boxes could be purchased from the grocery for five cents but buying them was considered a sinful extravagance since they as well as staples could be acquired by other means.

The planting of trees on Arbor Day was an annual event and was said to consist of some interesting ceremonies which I never attended as I had other and more important matters that demanded my attention. To most of us that occasion was merely a picnic on a large scale. It provided a day's outing in the open, a picnic lunch, and as many soft drinks as we could absorb, the quantity being limited by the amount of cash in hand. Picnics were almost a weekly occurence during the summer; a large number were conducted by the various churches, others by organizations, clubs, and large business houses—but we attended few of these as the church type was too restricted and the others were limited to special groups.

Coney Island, formerly Parker's or Parlor Grove was located on the Ohio River and was open to the public. Admission was twenty-five cents, including a round trip ride on a steam-boat. In its early inception it was a primitive affair. It had comparatively few attractions but one of these was the ancestor of the present roller-coaster. This was a double track affair, a straightaway, about forty feet high at each end. A loaded car took off at one end and the momentum would carry it almost to the top of the other end where an attendant was in waiting to provide the necessary motive power to carry it on to the top; the car would then be switched to the other track for the return journey. There were some stands vending hot dogs, ice cream, and soft drinks; a merry-go-round and a "knock the nigger baby down" outfit completed the picture.

That ice cream concession was held by Bacigalupo, who had an ice cream and oyster parlor on Sixth Street as his regular business. When the old man delivered half a dozen large ice cream freezers to the steam-boat for the excursion ride, his son Gus and I would help wheel them aboard; this chore accomplished, we forgot to come ashore and came into a round-trip boat ride for free. We seldom left the boat at Coney Island unless we were supplied with funds to indulge in the amusements afforded, which was not often.

Juvenile life in the Cincinnati of the Eighties was not all beer and skittles (whatever "skittles" are.) There were also duties then referred to as "chores" which formed a part of every growing boy's daily burden.

4
Chores

There were labors to be performed. While I was among the fortunate ones who had what was called "an allowance" any hint of unearned increment was noticeable by its absence. Mine was actually a salary and a meagre one at that, considering the amount of labor necessary to snare the fifteen to twenty-five cents per week I drew down. It cost me, by my estimate, some hundred dollars worth of time weekly at what for the most part I rated as unnecessary labor.

Our back and side yards were paved with brick which had to be scrubbed with a broom and properly rinsed every Saturday. This chore took up about an hour a week for each operation throughout the seven warm months of the year. In winter snow had to be carted out of the yard and deposited in the street. Why the snow had to be removed from the entire surface of the yards was a mystery to the youths who moved it. A path would have answered every purpose and in due time a benevolent providence would provide a warm spell and the snow would vanish with no expenditure of time or labor.

The hauling of coal from a shed in the back yard to the second floor in sufficient quantity to feed three stoves, and on special occasions a grate, was a necessary evil to which my youthful philosophy could find no objection in principle: I liked warmth but, having a congenital allergy to anything that remotely resembled work, I saved several hundred dollars worth per annum. I rigged up a pulley on the roof of the porch and, assisted by a chum who filled the bucket, coal was hauled up to the second floor with little labor and dumped into a large box on the back porch which held a week's supply. Still I really got the worst of the bargain, for I had to reciprocate and haul several buckets of coal from the cellar to the third floor of my chum's home, which did not sport a coal shed. My chum's family coal consumption was also inordinate: they had what they called their "laundry" located just under the roof, and the stove had to be fed once a week, winter and summer.

Errands of various kind also cut quite a swath from my leisure time. A trip from the grocery every so often with a five gallon can of coal oil for the oil stove which we used during the summer months was one of these. The can was hauled on a home-made wagon. Kindling had to be brought down from the attic, where a year's supply was stored. Water had to be drawn Sunday evening for Monday wash day. The water was dark brown, loaded with Ohio River mud, and it was necessary to draw enough on Sunday night, load each tub with an ounce of powdered alum and let it settle over-night. Alum was bought in chunks, placed in a cloth container and powdered with a hammer. Powdered alum may have been on the market but I had no knowledge of it: I powdered ours, from early youth to manhood. This was a tedious chore; the cloth would be worn through before the alum was reduced to powder and the mineral had to be decanted into another and more robust rag to complete the job.

Washer-women, white or colored, had a standard wage of one dollar per day for washing and ironing with breakfast and lunch as lagniappe—and they had to be substantial, if one wished to keep one's washer-woman. Clothes were dried in the yard on clotheslines during the summer, weather permitting; in winter the attic served.

Coffee, since it had to be purchased fresh from the grocery, also made a chore. It was purchased either at Frank's Grocery at Sixth and Race, or at another grocery several blocks north on Seventh Street. Why the change was in order every so often was a mystery to me: both supplied Rio coffee at prices varying from 23c to 25c per pound. So-called Mocha and Java sold for 30c.

When a ham or a slab of bacon was needed, it meant a trip to Court and Broadway to Davis's Packing Plant, a little over a mile from home for the family's errand boy. One type of bakery goods, coffee cake, came from Dunholter's Bakery on Sixth Street but bread had to be bought at Stewart's Bakery at Seventh and Race Streets. I once suggested to my mother that all these commodities could be had in one shop with a saving of time and sole leather, but I was promptly accused of harboring a selfish motive and my recommendation was tabled.

Carrying the market basket on Saturday afternoon was another boring proposition. The long-winded chaffering that was part of the buying agenda took up time I could have utilized in other and more profitable activities. The basket naturally got heavier with each purchase and I considered the dozen pretzels I received along the route in the way of remuneration inadequate. I felt that pretzels were only food and that I could have wangled them in some other way.

As a boy our author could see the worthwhile purpose of chores, even though he would willingly have excised them from his own personal program: there was another infringement upon his freedom in which he could see nothing but evil of the grossest sort.

Mrs. Smith's boy Willie had no patience whatever with Sunday School.

5
Years of Torture

The great calamity of my early youth occurred once a week, on Sunday. From the innocence of four until the mature age of thirteen, I attended Sunday School at the Methodist Episcopal Church on Ninth Street, about four blocks from my house. I was originally inveigled into this by the son of a saloon keeper, his father a tenant of ours, and the inducement was a bribe consisting of a rocking-horse with real hair.

This culprit disappeared a short time after my incarceration and in later years I reached the conclusion that he had made a compact with Satan to "spring him" and had cemented his bargain by leaving me as the sacrificial goat. This was the first and only bribe in my career; I plead guilty, but in extenuation I cite innocence, ignorance, and extreme youth. Time has remedied the last effect and innate depravity nullified the first two.

The Declaration of Independence is a dim and faded image of human glory on earth compared to the relief, the feeling of joy and freedom, I experienced when I at last escaped from this weekly servitude. True, it only lasted one and one half hours, from 2:30 to 4:00 P.M. but this afternoon session ruined my entire day, since my associates on Seventh Street all attended morning services and it was, for some occult reason, not considered kosher to associate with the otherwise blameless George Street crowd on Sunday. Why this distinction was in operation I never knew and it never occurred to me to question it: it was just one of those things.

The spiritual values acquired during these years in Sunday School were nil: on the practical side, I absorbed one valuable lesson which, later, was a factor in building up my bank account. On one occasion a special meeting was held in the church upstairs for the purpose of raising fifty thousand dollars, a large sum in those days. The Sunday School contingent was herded aloft to attend this meeting in the hope that they might among them produce a few shekels. We were lined up like a flock of sheep and escorted aloft to the main tent on the second floor, a holy of holies few of us had ever seen.

The pastor, Dr. B., opened his spiel with a request for a donation of twenty-five thousand. No dice. He then, by downgrading his demands and lingering for some time on each descending rung of the ladder, finally reached the sum of ten thousand. Hooray, he snared one! He hooked two more at seventy-five hundred. Glory be, he had half of it! He kept on lowering the boom on a graduated scale until he had the Sunday School contingent pledging amounts of fifty and twenty-five cents. When he hit this low level, I realized why we were there. He wasn't overlooking any bets: he played them win, place, and show, with the Sunday School captives as "also rans" good for an entry fee.

The moral of this lesson? Oh yes, there is a moral, likewise a priceless wad of sagacity which, if properly applied to mundane affairs, will pay dividends. In selling an article which is in stock in several grades, always show the highest priced item first. If the range is, say, from twenty-five to two hundred dollars, start with the highest and gradually climb down. When the buyer, poor fish, compares the two hundred dollar article which he cannot afford with the twenty-five dollar one, he will compromise at around seventy-five or one hundred. He probably cannot afford this either but pride keeps him in the higher bracket. If you start at twenty-five dollars and try to work up, you will scare the pants off him long before you reach the hundred dollar level.

About once a year the Methodist Church put on a grand show. An orgy called a revival was organized, usually with the aid of a professional sorcerer hired for the occasion. Such professionals usually worked on a commission basis, their remuneration being a cut of the so called free-will offerings or perhaps an appropriation guaranteed by the Board of Directors to the main spieler. If this was so at our church I had no knowledge of it; I was not consulted, although I was a stockholder contributing a few pennies regularly each week and more when a special drive was on the agenda.

A good barker could work up an emotional drunk in his audience in about fifteen minutes. One expert I remember made it in ten but the strain was too great; he collapsed the second day and the local talent had to take over. My Sunday School teacher, female of the species, wept over me during one of these orgies, using every brand of persuasion at her command to get me to mount the "mourner's bench," kneel, and confess my sins. Inasmuch as my sins were my own personal property, achieved by mine own efforts, I declined to share them with the congregation. There must have been some strain of mule in my make-up that saved me from making a complete ass of myself; I couldn't put up an argument so I just balked.

It was some time after one of these three ring circuses that our current Sunday School Superintendent tried to pull a fast one on the Bible Class of which I was a member at that time. This was an error on his part; it failed of its object and resulted in my release from bondage. He came up with a pledge for us to sign, pledging ourselves to use no likker, tobacco, or profanity. This at once put me down on three counts as I was addicted to all of them. I started to smoke at an early age, my folks served wine and beer on occasions and as for profanity, while I was as yet a mere tyro at this noble art, I had acquired a fair working knowledge. There were sixteen in our class, twelve of whom signed the pledge and immediately after leaving most of them lit up their cigarettes. The four black sheep did likewise but as we had had the moral grandeur to refuse the pledge we were not under wraps so there was no sin.

This Superintendent was a shiny-whiskered M.D. who labored with us for several weeks with no success, finally gave up and consigned us to the lower regions. He laid his lack of success to our innate depravtiy: he claimed we were plentifully supplied with it. The result of the pledge business was that the four of us rebels left the Sunday School and so far as I know none ever returned.

I can still recall our Superintendent's lecture on innate depravity, based on the original sin of old Adam. Our revered mentor insisted that we were not only in possession of a large stock of original sin, but also accused us of cultivating, nourishing, and fertilizing it, which no doubt accounts for its lasting so long. There is nothing equal to a good supply of innate depravity for maintaining original sin in a flourishing condition.

Meditating in later years, I have never been able to comprehend why such a minor peccadillo as stealing an apple, probably not ripe at that, should cast the blight of sin on the entire human race. If this sin was handed down and split up among the millions of human animals who have had their being since that time, it should by now be so attenuated and thinly spread over any one individual that it would take a Geiger counter to detect it.

If original sin is based on the theft of one apple, what glorious sinners we Cincinnati kids were—the looting of an apple cart was common practice and country boys had even greater opportunity to deviate, with whole orchards to prey upon. We probably had better apples at home but there was no adventure involved in getting them. We likewise made raids on such orchards as were convenient in the nearby hills though we usually arrived too early in the season and our loot consisted of green apples. We could not eat these, as we knew from experience the result would be disastrous, but it was lots of fun to appropriate them for a worthy purpose. We had no use for buckeyes either, though we hunted them in the fall of the year and, since they were rated as an efficient remedy for rheumatism, we carried one in the pants pocket just in case. There must have been some truth in this legend as I can't recall a single case of rheumatism among all the West End juveniles I knew.

My resignation from Sunday School entailed a sacrifice on my part that loomed large in my economy. In my mature years—say after my ninth—I had habitually exacted a percentage of all weekly and special donations for the heathen. I figured that, inasmuch as I was instrumental in collecting such funds, I was entitled to part of the loot. I had a very vague idea of what constituted a heathen anyway, and knew nothing of their needs or condition—but I was painfully aware that my allowance of twenty-five cents per week was inadequate for my wants in the way of tobacco and secondhand dime novels and that it had to be supplemented from some source.

Any boy addicted to reading in that day had his digestion imperiled by the printed propaganda distributed by the prolific church press and was forced to turn elsewhere for an antidote in order to preserve his health and thus save his family the pain that would presumably have accompanied his juvenile demise.

The productions of the House of Beadle saved many a life, as did Alger (perhaps you will not believe that Horatio Alger himself was once looked upon askance by some moralists), Ellis, Castlemon, and others. No matter what adults of that day may have thought of these works, the boy who encountered them was lucky: otherwise he might have become a subscriber to THE POLICE GAZETTE, with its Winchellesque gossip and its racy illustrations of chorus-girls in tights!

6
Literary Fare

The reading habits of the denizens of George and Sixth Streets call for no comment as they were non-existent. Such reading as was indulged in by the youth of my time was confined to that region of higher culture, Seventh Street. There all grades of literature were represented and covered a wide field, from the lowest, books borrowed from the Sunday School Library, to those procured from the Cincinnati Public Library. The space between this literary sandwich was graced with the good red meat of Beadle's dime and half-dime novels, the Wide Awake Library, Old Cap Collier, and similar lively fare. These provided the stuffing for the sandwich, and it could be seasoned with the mustard of such weekly papers as *The Boys of New York* and *The Young Men of America.*

Golden Days also had a large circulation. The tales in this periodical were not as lurid as the type of story found in *The Boys of New York,* being of a more conservative type on the general order of Ellis, Alger, Castlemon [whose real name was Fosdick, as in Harry Emerson] et al. They also featured in each issue a Sunday School lesson which took up one entire page. This was bait calculated to avoid any possible censorship by parent, teacher, or free-lance reformer and was looked upon by youthful readers as a sinful waste of good space.

Beadle's novels were contraband but one could sneak by with *The Boys of New York* and *The Young Men of America,* which carried the same type of story found in Beadle's quite often by the same writers, but did not nominate themselves "novels." Such foolish people as parents and Sunday School teachers, somehow became innoculated with the idea that "dime novels" were instruments of Satan, while anything in the way of a weekly or monthly periodical was, if not entitled to a halo, at least surrounded with an aura of respectability. The fact is that none of those elders ever looked critically at either medium: if they had, the likeness would have been so obvious that anyone with the brain of a Piltdown man would have spotted it immediately.

There were several dealers in Cincinnati who carried Beadle's and other novels as published, with a considerable stock of earlier and slightly used issues. The main source of supply for new copies was Spinney's on Sixth Street near Race. They had several hundred in stock, which were all sold for the list-price as new. A number of other dealers, widely scattered about the city, specialized in used copies which they offered at half price: these also operated an exchange system whereby the customer could trade in two for one: two half-dime used issues for one full dime type.

The largest dealer in dime novels was one "Doc" K———. "Doc" was a courtesy title: he could read—some, at least. He was a disreputable old fossil who operated a junk shop on Central Avenue between Sixth and George Streets and his premises were stocked with about five hundred old books, mostly trash, and a large assortment of Beadle's, Wide Awakes, and others of the same breed. He sold them at half of the list price and also ran an exchange. As an additional convenience to the young and impecunious he likewise dispensed penny pieces of eating tobacco. He was wont to cut a dime plug into fifteen thin slices and dispose of them for a penny each, thereby adding fifty per cent to his normal profit. As my allowance at the time ranged from fifteen to twenty-five cents per week, depending upon the state of rectitude I had recently demonstrated at home, I was often forced to patronize Doc's gyp market when the bargain price of an entire plug exceeded the total of my financial resources.

Contemporary with Beadle's in the field of literary offerings was the Wide Awake Library, already mentioned, which featured a type of story entirely different. Wide Awake content was largely of the comic variety but it appealed to the same clientele. There was nothing in the Wide Awake about the wild west, Indians, or outlaws which were the mainstay subject of Beadle's; instead three of the Wide Awake writers ran a series of stories depicting the same characters in various situations. One series related the adventures of "Skinny the Tin Pedlar" and his kicking mule. (Youthful readers sometimes twisted this title to bring out a more esoteric meaning.) Another series by "Noname" featured, as the main character, one Frank Read who was the inventor of the Steam Horse, the Steam Man, the Electric Boat, the Electric Wagon, and finally the Airship. The Electric Wagon was pictured as an ordinary type vehicle but without shafts, as no horses were required, with a top consisting of a bullet proof wire screen with loopholes strategically located so that enemies could be exterminated in safety. The Airship was depicted on the front of the novel as an ordinary flat-bottomed boat with two masts stepped into the deck, at the head of which was an object that resembled an inverted electric fan called, by the author, a "ratascope." This twirler provided the lifting power while another at the stern drove the contraption horizontally. It was a prophetic vision of the helicopter of to-day but the author will probably collect no royalties. Possibly he is dead.

On the comic side, Wide Awake ran a series entitled the "Shorty Stories." The characters of the triumvirate featured as heroes were depicted on the cover by a crude wood-cut in three sizes. Short Shorty the grandfather, always referred to as the "Old Man" was the largest of these. Second in order was his son, simply called "Shorty," and the third, and naturally shortest, was a grandson called "The Kid." Their adventures were recorded in a large number of issues until a final great calamity broke the family into such minute fragments that their creator, recognizing the mess he had created, threw in the sponge and the series was discontinued.

There was no Einstein at the time and the Philadelphia lawyers, after viewing the situation, ran for cover so the relationship which follows is still an unsolved mystery. When the three characters next appeared, the son, Shorty, married a widow with two daughters, one of whom married the grandfather, Short, and the other the grandson, The Kid. This made the grandson the brother-in-law of the grandfather and the son was the father-in-law of the grandfather. Relegate your cross word puzzles to the attic and spend the rest of your time on earth tracing the various ramifications involved in this genealogical mess.

Weekly papers were regular reading the year round; dime novels were mainly summer reading, as they could be perused out-doors away from all forms of censorship, but were sometimes read in winter during school hours, concealed behind a geography which was the only school book large enough to hide them.

During the winter season we leaned more heavily on the Cincinnati Public Library. This was located on Vine Street about four blocks from home. I would meet a chum of mine, Frank Smith, about seven in the evening to trek to the Public Library in search of something by Ellis, Alger, or Fosdick. The system of distribution in the Library was primitive and at times our patience was sorely tried. On one side of the stairs leading to the reading room was a counter on which was displayed a catalogue from which we could make a selection of wanted items. A list giving the shelf number of the titles wanted was made out and handed to an attendant at the end of the room and we customers then adjourned to the other side of the stairway to the delivery desk. The books came down in a small elevator, later in a chute, one's card number would be called and the books delivered. Sometimes several of our lists would be returned marked "out" and as each attempt involved about ten minutes' time we would give up the ghost and mark a list "anything by Ellis" trusting in Providence to snare one we had not read.

Stories and so-called lives of the James boys and the Younger Brothers were current but we saw little of them: they purported to be factual stories and thus lacked the glamour of fiction for us—besides they were usually priced at fifty cents to a dollar so that even secondhand copies at half price were beyond our reach. I did snare between thirty and forty copies of the earlier yellow back Beadle's issued in the Sixties and early Seventies and old dog-robber Doc K—— charged the full price, ten cents, for these issues on the ground that they were rare, which they no doubt were.

Keeping track of a dozen continued stories in three or four weekly papers, with some Beadle publications and library books each week, was a full-time job that had to be switched in between such other chores as eating, going to school, and sleeping, with time out for other activities: but by concentration and devious means I got it done. The same amount of effort applied to some gainful operation to-day would make me a millionaire: all I got out of it was a liberal education.

The novels of Mary J. Holmes, M. E. Braddon, Julie Smith, and E. D. E. N. Southworth constituted the romance consumed by the adult population. The weekly issues of the *Family Story Paper, The Fireside Companion* and *The New York Ledger* served as current literature for the grown-ups. Such papers were known as "throw-aways," since they were passed out on market days as free samples in the hope that the reader would be intrigued with some of the stories and would purchase succeeding issues.

Eating is a pastime that has always been popular with our author: it is still at the present—his eighty-seventh year—and is likely to continue so. In the interval of better than four score years since he first became aware of its importance to human welfare, he has become something of an authority on the subject. Obviously, from the following, he had come to know his way about Cincinnati eating establishments while still in knee pants.

7
Eating Habits

Food supplies at that time were limited in variety but plentiful in quantity. Rabbit food, in the shape of cereals processed and packaged, did not exist. Only two kinds of cereals were available, cracked wheat and rolled oats. These were sold in bulk, openly displayed in large wooden bowls, and the price was five cents per pound: about right, I suppose, allowing something to the merchant for scooping them up. Such comestibles were boiled until tender and served with milk and sugar. A doctor writing a series of articles on food for a local paper of the day stated that there was more food value in a rasher of bacon than in a pound of cereal—which was only fit for consumption by rabbits, as they could eat it neat.

Within a radius of three or four blocks from Seventh and Central Avenues were located a dozen or more groceries and about half that number of bakeries. Grocery stores were present in considerable variety, ranging from a little hole in the wall with a very limited stock to two representatives of early chains, located on Sixth Street, the Atlantic and Pacific Tea Company and the Hamilton Grocery Company. Hamilton's was a local chain of three stores located on Pearl, Sixth, and Court Streets, all of these being streets where triweekly markets were held. Hamilton's was the largest grocery on Sixth Street, employing a manager at fifteen dollars per week (every week), two clerks, and a lady cashier, with an additional clerk on Saturday, an afternoon market day on which the store did not close until ten at night.

Hamilton's had quite a suburban trade and made delivery by wagon to a different suburb each day from Monday to Friday. When deliveries were made, orders were taken for the following week and such orders were filled each evening between seven and nine for the next day's delivery. Few items were packaged. Perhaps there were a dozen in all, used by the average family, including various fruits, peas, corn, and cove oysters in cans: practically everything else came in bulk. Oil or molasses had to be drawn out of a barrel, cheese had to be cut and weighed, butter came in firkins and was weighed and placed in a wooden dish for family use, lard was dug out of a tierce and placed in the same receptacle that served for butter. Coffee was housed in bins and had to be weighed and sometimes ground, unless the customer preferred to grind his own. In case some sybarite wanted it powdered, the labor of two men was required to turn the big wheel on the grinder, and five minutes of hard labor was necessary from them. The comments of the operators on such occasions "Ain't fit to be written and much less read."

Sugar, the granulated variety, was easy; all types of sugar came in five hundred pound barrels and the granulated product could be scooped out of the barrel with little effort. Coffee "A" sugar, and the dark brown type, necessitated the use of a two-pronged augur to ready it for the scoop, while lump sugar, as it was called, demanded a four-pronged rake and getting it out of the cask was a tough job at that.

Tea, housed in fancy tin canisters, was doled out in quantities ranging from one-quarter to one-half pound lots, weighed and wrapped. Pepper, spices, dried peas, beans, and dozens of other items required weighing and wrapping. "Fancy" table salt came in five-pound cloth bags, but the cheaper and coarser variety in barrels also had to be weighed.

These statistics are not based on mere observation. I learned hard facts on the occasions when I made an extra hand at Hamilton's during periods of rush and stress before holidays. A chum of mine, Johnny Casey, was the junior clerk at Hamilton's and his chore was putting up, between seven and nine in the evening, the suburban orders for the next morning's delivery. Once or twice a week I served without pay in order to shorten Johnny's servitude by one hour. For a week before Christmas I helped wait on trade and fill orders of evenings from four until nine, for which I collected the then enormous sum of one dollar per diem.

Dunholter's Bakery on Sixth Street was the best in our immediate neighborhood, with Stewart's at Seventh and Race Streets carrying a larger and fancier variety of bakery goods, featuring cream puffs and cream rolls that sold two for five cents and can now be purchased at ten cents and two-for-a-quarter each, though the quality is not up to the old standard.

The smaller type of grocery carried some items not handled in the larger stores; milk in bulk, for instance, which could be had at three cents per pint, quarts—five cents. Most bulk milk was delivered by dairies that ran wagons over regular routes in the manner of today. A wagonload then comprised a dozen five gallon cans of loose milk which was bailed out with a tin dipper attached to a long handle and then poured into the receptacle in the waiting hands of the consumer. Such delivery men rang a bell to notify their customers of their arrival. In cases where there was no response to the bell and the driver had a definite order to leave milk, he found some sort of open container placed on the stoop or doorstep, decanted into it the required quantity and left it there. If the purchaser did not promptly take it in, it sometimes provided dessert for a thirsty dog or a predatory cat.

While there were a number of butcher shops on Sixth Street, most of the meat consumed there was handled in the old Market House, predecessor of the present edifice. This house, one block in length, was lined inside with two rows of stalls on market days. The butchers occupied about three-quarters of the space, and the balance, devoted to the sale of fish, was located at the Central Avenue end. The odorous fog created by the fish covered several blocks.

Open markets were held on Sixth Street four days each week; Monday, Wednesday, and Friday mornings, and Saturday afternoons—the latter lasting well into the evening. The market stalls then covered three city blocks, from Elm to John Streets, and the area was occupied by various distributors of edibles. These stands had a definite location, each being licensed by the city. An attempt to describe the numerous enterprises located in these three blocks would make a chapter by itself so I will confine the record to a description of a few unusual specimens.

Foremost, to my juvenile eye, was the hominy man, a tall Negro with a two-foot top piece of white cloth for a hat, and a large container containing hominy. Burning charcoal at the bottom of the can kept the commodity warm. I can still hear his call "hominy hot." Then there was the horseradish vendor; he operated a machine built on the line of the old itinerant scissors-grinders and operated by foot power. A small glass of his product cost five cents and with salt and vinegar added made an excellent relish. One could see him grind the article and know there were no turnips used as a filler.

The pretzel man on the corner, with a washbasket full of his produce, tendered pretzels ten for five cents, the price for either the complex kind or the straight banana shaped type.

One stand carried nothing but tripe.

Butter stands were much in evidence. Their product was offered in rolls running five or six pounds each. A knife was handed to the prospective purchaser with a modicum of butter on the end and after sampling several kinds, a decision would be made and the purchase concluded. (There was only one knife in use and after having been licked by forty or fifty customers it was probably thoroughly contaminated.) The required amount of the article was then cut from the roll with a looped wire, weighed and delivered.

Smoked meats and sausages of various kinds were offered in great variety: weiners, bologna, blut-wurst, knack-wurst, and many others, all of them items not handled by the more elegant butchers in the Market House.

The sauerkraut man was there, dishing out his succulent product in different sized wooden boats, such as were used for butter and lard in bulk, with a five or ten cent price tag according to size.

The cheeseman was a prominent feature on the scene. Cheddar was called "New York something or other." There was also local cheddar, and a variety of odd cheeses winding up with hand kase, a product whose odor ran a hot competition with the fish market; they had schmierkase, the old smooth type, and retaining all the flavor of the lactic acid. It was sold for five cents a pint. Season this with salt and pepper, add a sprinkling of schnittlauch, slice an onion, place the structure on a slab of dark rye bread, and you had a luxury not obtainable in these degenerate days. The illegitimate mess called "cottage cheese" offered for sale to-day is a manufactured article in the same category as blended whiskey.

An arm of the open market ran north on Plum Street from Sixth to Seventh Streets and the stands there were not rented by the city but were reserved for the use of farmers who brought their produce to town in wagons, arriving there early in the morning and remaining until sold out. This block was a happy hunting ground for people with limited funds and also for the more conservative who bought in quantity lots for storage, canning, pickling, and preserving for use in winter.

In addition to common farm produce one could find in that area many out-of-the-way items that grew wild, that were gathered by the farmer contingent and brought to market. There were such items as hazel nuts (filberts to-day), walnuts, hickory nuts, butternuts, pawpaws, persimmons, the fruit of the locust tree, wild honey, and herbs of various kinds. Those were the condiments that afforded flavor to the standard products.

Tomatoes and potatoes sold for fifty cents the bushel. Green corn cost ten cents per dozen, berries and fruits in season came at prices that enabled the thrifty householder to put by a winter's supply without undue strain on the exchequer.

The more opulent of the vicinity utilized this source of supply to lay by their winter needs. Flour was bought from the grocery at around five dollars a barrel, which held one hundred and ninety-six pounds. Winter apples came by the barrel; several bushels of potatoes and two bushels of tomatoes, one for canning and one for catsup, were normal purchases from the farm block. With these, a whole ham, and a slab of bacon on hand, the average household could have held out a month, even if *all* supplies were cut off.

Street vendors operating push carts offered such rare and exotic delicacies as oranges, lemons, bananas, hot roasted chestnuts, peanuts, and hokey pokey ice cream. This so-called ice cream was a mixture of milk, sugar, cornstarch and coloring matter: it had the merit of reducing the temperature but offered very little food value—a much better grade was sold by John Bacigalupo, who ran the ice cream and oyster palace on Sixth Street, but the best was made by Alfred Ransley, located on Central Avenue. His price was fifty cents per quart and it more nearly resembled a decent grade of the modern article.

The restaurants in the West End were third or fourth rate, only cheap joints where one could put his feet in the trough and absorb what provender he needed for the small sum of twenty-five cents. Evening meals ranged slightly higher, the price being around forty cents. Such an evening menu provided an entree, potatoes, one vegetable, dessert, and coffee.

Meals to order ran somewhat higher. The language in use by West End waiters in transmitting their orders through a hole in the the wall to the cook was colorful, possibly deserving of study by philologists: a steak was a "slaughter in the pan," coffee, "a muddy," scrambled eggs on toast, "Adam and Eve on a raft, wreck 'em," eggs fried on one side, "sunnyside up," etc. Such restaurants lasted well into the present century; I can recall one on Sixth Street, just east of Vine Street, that had quite an elaborate menu; meat courses fifteen cents, potatoes, vegetables, coffee, and dessert five cents each. I occasionally patronized this joint as a matter of convenience as I had a branch store that was open evenings in the vicinity. On leaving the place one evening I was braced by a panhandler who gave me the usual song and dance. I told him I would not give him money but would feed him. To my surprise he took me at my word and I took him into the place and gave the cashier the promise that I would pay later. When I came back to settle I was confronted with a check to the amount of eighty-five cents and while I paid the tab cheerfully, I regretted that I had not been present to watch him stow away its value in rations. My capacity even in those days of youth, was usually limited to forty cents at that joint.

Some of the bakeries put out a limited breakfast or lunch consisting of coffee and sinkers (doughnuts) which set the buyer back five cents; this with a cut of pie at the same price stacked up enough calories to keep the wheels turning until something of a more solid nature could be lined up. Bread sold for five cents a loaf in most bakeries; Stewart's on Seventh Street charged ten cents but even their price could be reduced by buying the "bread tickets" they offered, which bought three loaves for twenty-five cents.

Although any oldster of orthodox pattern is willing to swear that everyone worked harder, longer, and more efficiently in the Old Days, Mr. Smith seems to recall a good deal of social activity in the Eighties that must have required time off from labor by the participants.

Mr. Smith is definitely not orthodox but perhaps there were more hours in the Cincinnati day than elsewhere—or possibly he was simply invited out more than most of those who now prefer to sigh for the past rather than live in the present, as he does.

8
Social Customs

Social customs and the home life of the middle-income and more opulent denizens of the near West End, were simple and primitive. But on the whole, from the standpoint of ease and comfort, they were more conducive to a satisfying evening than the rat races of to-day. Gossip, as in all ages and times, was a part of the agenda but perhaps social intercourse on the whole was on a higher plane than obtains in the present frenzied era. What with television, radio, moving pictures, and the comic supplements in the newspapers, culture to-day has sunk to a new low.

The residents in the higher brackets had "at home" days but most of the calling was of a more casual order, of which I shall have more to say later. Any time in the afternoon or evening might come a ring at the door announcing a visitor, or perhaps a group of friends or relatives. After some exchange of gossip and slander the conversation became more general; politics, the current literature of the period, anything unusual in the way of world news, and last but not least, the Civil War. This topic wore well even into the latter Eighties. Literary discussion among the hoi polloi was confined to criticism of such classics as the works of Augusta Evans, E.D.E.N.

Southworth, Julie Smith, M. E. Braddon, and Mary J. Holmes.

Any visitor dropping in late in the afternoon was invited to stay for the evening meal; the larder was always well stocked and an additional guest or two was no problem. As we have noted, the average household was well calculated to stand a siege of some duration.

There were also semi-public or at least neighborhood gatherings in the cause of social intercourse. Unhappily many of these were church-sponsored, and thus had a shadow cast upon their motivation. Anyone with the necessary twenty-five cents was welcome whether or not he was a member of the sect sponsoring the affair. For this small sum, church organizations offered a bounteous quantity of contributed refreshments. (If anyone wished to see a housewife's supreme effort in the Eighties, he had only to ask her to bake a cake for a church social: that did it.) All the food provided was contributed by female members of the church who also officiated as waitresses and thus made a net profit of one hundred per cent of the price. In addition, there was a hidden profit wrapped up in the deal; the captive audience was forced to listen to lengthy opening and closing prayers, with a talk from a visiting missionary providing the meat for the ecclesiastical sandwich.

German bands seldom played the West End circuit; nearly all their activities took place in the northern part of the city, known as "Over the Rhine," where the population was ninety per cent German. One German band, a one man affair, was a whole team with a "hoss" to let and a dog under the wagon. He played four instruments at once; with one hand he fingered a horn of sorts, something like a cornet, with the other he tapped a triangle and on his back was a miniature bass drum and a pair of cymbals; these were operated with a cord attached to the heel of one of his shoes. When the drum part was in order, he stood one one hind leg and kicked with the other one. So far as I know he lasted but one season but even that was quite an achievement for one man doing four men's work.

I cannot recall that the Methodist Church, whose Sunday School served as my jail for an hour and thirty minutes each Sunday, ever sponsored a picnic. However, I attended several given by other denominations in our neighborhood, having been invited by one of my chums who was a member. These were stodgy affairs; there were too many watch dogs. The entire force of Sunday School teachers was always present and was supplemented by the preacher, the Sunday School Superintendent, and all the elders and deacons. Under this Argus-eyed aggregation there was little chance to indulge in pleasant activities, all of which were frowned upon by those in authority.

Some time during the Eighties Arbor Day was instituted. It was an annual tree-planting affair which developed into a city-wide picnic; all schools were closed and for weeks ahead we were encouraged put by our pennies and nickels for the occasion. The affair was held in Eden Park, the largest open area in town. For five cents the entrance of the park could be reached by horse-drawn cars; but as the distance from down town was only about two miles, many of the young fry walked and thereby were ahead by one bottle of "pop" or sarsaparilla. Sausages, now called hot-dogs, could be had for the sum of five cents. They were split lengthwise, placed between two large slabs of rye bread, and deluged with mustard. A half dozen of these washed down with as many bottles of the liquid as our means allowed provided many a stomach ache for young nature lovers. The hot-dogs of that era were longer and thicker than those of to-day and the bread was cut from a loaf of a larger size; two of them would make a fair meal for a man while six were just about right for a boy in his teens. Three types of soft drinks were available, mineral water, sarsaparilla, and strawberry, the latter composed of water, sugar, and some sort of dye material: the only resemblance to a strawberry was the color. Hokey pokey was also available to the unwary.

Lectures, magic lantern shows, and magicians often held forth in the several small halls in our neighborhood, halls with a seating capacity limited to not more than one hundred and fifty.

One fakir rented a small hall over a saloon at the southeast corner of Ninth and Plum Streets. He passed out dodgers among the school children announcing a show by a magician at which prizes were to be distributed at the end of the performance: a barrel of flour was the top prize and admission was fifteen cents. I squandered that amount out of curiosity, as I had never seen a magician perform, but I came out disillusioned. A few tricks such as I had often seen executed by street hawkers—tricks with a coin, a handkerchief, cards and an egg—comprised the entire show. This was followed by an announcement that his shipment of prizes had been delayed in transit! Even so, unless he bilked the owner out of the rent for the hall, I can't see how he paid for his printing and other expenses. His audience, less than sixty kids at fifteen cents per head, ran to something under nine dollars.

Several of the boys in the neighborhood owned magic lanterns and gave shows for which they demanded a penny, but as their audience was limited and the per capita wealth of local juveniles was a minus quantity, none of them ever retired to live on unearned increment. Shows of this kind on a larger scale were often presented in one of the halls in the West End. In these professional productions geographical, historical, and other scenes were shown. Such exhibits were advertised by a barker who assumed the title "professor." He stood next to the cloth screen and after rattling off each description would call out, "Larry, turn the crank," when his assistant would run in another slide. His spiel was often parodied by the more sophisticated of that generation and such parodies in time trickled down to the lower age levels and provided amusement for youths of the mature age of thirteen. It is regrettable that such parodies cannot be circulated in this degenerate age, but it would be dangerous—since they have barred *Huckleberry Finn* in New York, deleted the word "nigger" from *Old Man River* and *Old Black Joe*, forbidden any reference of a ribald nature to Lawyers, Doctors, Dutch, Irish, Scotch, and others who must necessarily remain nameless to avoid prosecution. Comstockery is with us again, with improvements that Old Anthony never conceived in his wildest dreams. I was under the impression that the puritanical libido for regulating the affairs of their betters had been relegated to the wilds of Kansas and Nebraska (with branches in Iowa and Missouri) and entertained great hopes that when it crossed the Rockies and hit a civilized city like San Francisco it would be liquidated and buried in potter's field, or get lost among the hen-house sects of Los Angeles. Alas, it's almost back home.

Christmas and New Year's days were turkey days. Turkeys then sold for around ten cents per pound, and a twelve pound specimen was about right for a sitting of six people; that is, grown folks. For teenagers say around four would be a better estimate. As our family consisted of at most three and later but one adult and one minor, we always had to scout around to find some unattached people whom we could invite for the occasion. The bird we had was usually stuffed with dressing made of stale bread, eggs, onions, and sage. Some sybarites used chestnuts or oysters but we never rose to such heights. For side dishes the local custom required mashed potatoes, a vegetable, salad and last but not least, mince pie, served hot. Cranberry sauce was a must. The Jewish residents in the vicinity paid a sort of token attention to the holidays, but their taste ran to goose rather than turkey as the main dish. I once dined with a Jewish family who served roast goose stuffed with sauerkraut: it didn't work out—ruined the kraut.

New Year's Day was also a gala occasion; nearly all the population in the middle and upper classes kept what was termed "open house." On that day, if no other, wine, beer, whiskey, punch, and egg-nog comprised the liquid refreshments. These were flanked by a layout of small cakes, sliced meat, sausage, cheese, baked ham; all in such variations as occurred to the hostess. Egg-nog was almost a must and the combination of rich milk, sugar, eggs, brandy, and rum was quite a factor in the doctor's income for the following week. The German population usually served wine and a variety of German cakes—lebkuchen, springerle, and pfeffernusle—their affairs were correspondingly popular and the results tremendously painful.

The caravan of callers took off early in the afternoon: it continued until its members could no longer navigate or remember the address of the next place of call.

New Year's was a grand orgy followed, for all but the most robust, by a week of repentance.

And then there was what we called just plain, informal "visiting" —a harmless and pleasant pastime if ever there was one, for all concerned.

My earliest recollections date back to the time I was between three and four years old, when my grandfather, Philip Rittweger, began to tote me around with him on his excursions to various parts of the city and suburbs, calling on his old German friends. Such calls were informal, without any advance notice; if, as sometimes happened, there was no one at home, a short trek on foot or a twenty minutes ride on a horse-car would provide a second chance.

These visits were always made in the afternoon between two and four-thirty. After the usual greetings, which were always made while standing on our hind legs, we were invited to sit and in a few minutes the hostess would appear with a pot of coffee and a tray of small cakes. The coffee was available at all times. A gallon coffee pot was kept on the back of the stove where it would stay hot without boiling. When the supply ran low, a handful of coffee was thrown into the pot and some water added. This rejuvenating process continued until the pot was filled with coffee grounds, then it was emptied and a fresh concoction was in order. Egg shells were a part of the mixture; they were supposed to clarify the liquid. All coffee was run through a strainer to eliminate the coffee grounds before serving. When the pot was nearly full, the resulting liquid served not only as a beverage but would also have made a good varnish remover.

Most of the calls I made with Grandfather were in the near West End and in the German quarter, "Over the Rhine," all of them within easy walking distance. Several of his friends resided in the suburbs and one outside the city limits on Madison Road about one mile this side of Oakley. To reach this *ultima thule* required two hours' time each way so such visits were made in the morning with the return trip around four o'clock in the afternoon. This trek involved an hour's ride on the Elm Street horse-car line to the car barns in the east part of the city. At that point we transferred to what was known as a "dummy." This bone-shaker was an elongated street car with a small compartment in front which housed a boiler, an engine, a pile of coal and an engineer. The seats ran the length of the car, with passengers sitting back-to-back, as cards in a game of stud poker. The track was narrow-gauge and the side motion added at least fifty per cent to the length of the ride. The dummy ran from the East End car barns to Delta Station on the Pennsylvania Railroad, where it separated into two lines, one of them running to Columbia, the other to Mt. Lookout. Our destination was Mt. Lookout, from which point we had a mile walk on a mud road.

Another long trip was a trek we sometimes made to Ludlow, Kentucky. This involved a walk of over a mile on Fifth Street to the Ludlow Ferry which crossed the Ohio River at that point. It was another all day affair. The family we visited at Ludlow had about two acres of ground including a garden and an orchard. The rear fence ran along the bank of the Ohio River and for a youngster the river, with its occasional steamboat, was a fascinating sight. The heavy meal of the day, called dinner, was served at noon: it included soup, meat, vegetables and dessert, usually pie of some kind. Beer or wine was served to grease the skids and as an aid and encouragement to digestion.

A home on Brown Street, now McMicken Avenue, was a regular place of call for us. The back yard of this place verged on the canal and was located about one and one-half miles from our house. In good weather we walked, as twenty cents car-fare for a round trip of this short distance was an unthinkable extravagance—it was the price of a "T" bone steak or two pounds of pork chops.

Once every week the old gentleman would make a safari to an Over the Rhine wine house. I cannot recall just where this was located but I have a clear recollection of the interior and the appearance of the members of a sort of informal club who met there once a week. There were perhaps a dozen in the group, of which some six or seven was the usual quota for a meting. They sat around a long table and drank either Rhine or Moselle wine. Each individual ordered what he wished and paid for it on delivery with a small gratuity to the waiter: there was no treating. The wine was served in what was called a shoppen—a glass holding about six ounces, similar to the glasses of the present time in use for Old Fashioned cocktails. Such servings cost twenty or twenty-five cents each, depending on the type of wine ordered. From the time I was four years old, my portion was a half shoppen, and that was my quota for the entire session. The oldsters imbibed from three to six shoppens and were at times in a mellow mood by the end of the meeting. It is perhaps just as well that I was limited to a half portion: more would probably have started me on the downward path to a drunkard's grave. My grandfather's idea of the value of money saved me from such a parlous end. When one of the members had a birthday, wine was brought to the table in bottles and on such occasions nearly the entire coterie was present and the usual limit was disregarded.

Conversation at these gatherings was mostly in German with an occasional lapse into English for the benefit of a few of the second generation contingent whose German was limited or absent The subject was mainly the old way of life in Germany compared to conditions in America, tales of the Schwartswald (Black Forest), ghost stories, and Old World superstitions—with a heavy seasoning of American politics. Those who attended were, with one exception, Republicans, so the lone Democrat had hard sledding. Philosophy and religion were topics that stuck their heads above the horizon at times but such were not overly popular with the majority who considered them palpable nonsense and an uncalled for interference with their libations. I had excellent opportunity to acquire a knowledge of the German lingo but as there were several dialects in use, with only two members who used "hoch deutsch" it was a mixed dish and I got but little culture out of it. My grandfather spoke the Wurtemburg dialect naturally. He could, on occasion, make a stab at the high German when he thought such an effort necessary but it was a painful operation and always left a bad taste in his mouth; and at that, his foot would slip every so often and out would jump in a word or phrase that was pure dialect.

One member of the assembly named Flammer, who had come to America only some ten years before, was a disgruntled specimen and damned the country because during his short stay he had not succeeded in acquiring a million dollars. His favorite expression was "das Gottverdamte Amerika." After several sessions at which he voiced his discontent, Grandfather hit the ceiling: he rose in his chair, and calling the gentleman by name, said, in German, "Flammer, I knew your people in Germany. They were tenants; they didn't own land. They were poor; if they had meat once a week they were fortunate. When a pig was killed in the neighborhood, they were on hand with a bowl for the blood to make "blutwurst." You say you don't like it here. Come down town with me and I'll buy you a ticket and you can go back to Germany."

Needless to say the offer was not accepted and neither did the gentleman appear at subsequent meetings.

Several years after Grandfather's demise, my mother made arrangements for me to spend two weeks with some German relatives who operated a farm about two miles from Loveland, Ohio. We had just returned from our annual visit to Germantown, Ohio, so why my mother wanted to get shut of me for two weeks I could not comprehend but she probably had a good reason. She was right in this move, whatever her motives. At the age of twelve my theological knowledge concerning heaven and other localities displayed in our Sunday School geography was dim: when I got back from Loveland, I had a concrete idea of what heaven really was, or at least what it should be if I were permitted to draw up the plans and specifications. These sound Christian relatives of ours had reduced good living down to an exact science.

They arose at six, stowed away a substantial breakfast and went to work. At nine in the morning, they laid off for a fifteen minute interval and laid in a supply of sausage and cheese, washed down with beer or hard cider. At noon, they really went to town with a six course meal. Three o'clock in the afternoon brought a repetition of the morning lay-off. Six o'clock post meridian, was supper time (so called) and around nine in the evening, before going to bed, they served up a snack—something light, usually a chunk of pie. Six meals a day, every day, and all of them lived to be a good old age. That proved something, to my young mind. I still believe it.

Another port-of-call for a two or three weeks visit every summer was Germantown, recently mentioned.

The farmers in that region, one of the richest in the state, constantly complained: nothing was ever right. The weather was wrong, crops were bad, prices for their produce were too low—everything they had to buy was high in price. From the age of six until I reached the mature age of ten, I felt sorry for them. Then I began to figure that people who had three kinds of pie for breakfast and were able to send all their brats to college must be collecting my sympathy under false pretenses: to-day I think *all* American farming—judging by newspaper reports and government action—must be in the hands of descendants, or at least disciples, of those Germantown farmers of my boyhood!

Hopeful candidates for the degree of Master of Arts, or even Doctor of Philosophy, have from time to time devoted scholarly research to the subject of "The Theatre in Cincinnati." Some, possibly all, of these earnest young persons undoubtedly managed to put together some document in typescript to which their bored preceptors could not object and they received the letters they coveted.

But there have been other, more authentic, accounts of the doings of the disciples of Thespis in the Queen City. Sol Smith acted on the Cincinnati boards very early in the Nineteenth Century and later wrote about his experiences. Our Smith, William C., actually attended performances (when the price appeared to him to be right) in the theatre of his time—and was not averse to taking in a minstrel show, a "Tom Show," or watching a patent medicine sales-pitch. He also classified certain street-vendors as entertainers, and therefore Thespians—and quite properly, by any standards except those of the most precious and unduly dedicated.

9
Entertainment

Two theatres, Havlin's Theatre on Central Avenue and Robinson's Opera House at Ninth and Plum Streets, provided entertainment for the four hundred of our vicinity. Havlin's specialized in old-fashioned melodrama while Robinson's operated on a somewhat higher plane, presenting plays of the more sophisticated kind and such musical shows as were produced by Susie Kirwin's Opera Company, which played there one entire season.

Minstrel shows were popular and "Uncle Tom's Cabin" was performed at least once a year in one or both of these houses.

For the *hoi polloi,* magic lantern shows, prestidigitators, lecturers, on various topics, phrenologists, religious fanatics, and tight-rope walkers were on the menu every year. Such performances for the herd were held in one or another of what were called "Halls"—usually a large room above a saloon.

The only tight-rope walker I can recall viewing was distinguished in that he had but one leg. An inch-and-a-half rope was stretched across Central Avenue between the second floors of opposite buildings and a crutch, hollowed out to accommodate itself to the rope, did duty as a second leg. He mushed back and forth several times while his stooges milled about among the crowd passing the hat for voluntary contributions. Reading "the riot act" is the official method for dispersing a crowd: passing the hat is more efficient.

Sixth Street from Central Avenue to Elm Street was more than twice as wide as the average street. The block between Central Avenue and Plum Street was taken up by a market house, while the block between Plum and Elm Streets has already been described as part of the open square reserved for farmers and locally known as the "Hay Market." There farmers anchored their wagons loaded with hay to await a buyer, having had the hay weighed at the city scales located at the Elm Street end. Other farm products were wholesaled in this block, usually to the commission houses that lined the north side of the thoroughfare. This wide space dedicated to commerce during the day, was unoccupied in the evening and a camping ground for various types of fakirs, medicine men, political highbinders, and religious fanatics of all tints and breeds.

The average medicine man usually operated from a small stand—perhaps an open suitcase set on a folding frame—without any special display. He depended on his patter to put over his product. Such patter, compounded with a sure knowledge of the mental capacity of his audience, was well adapted to hold the attention of the crowd most likely to invest in his wares. He gave a running commentary about nothing in particular, interspersed occasionally with a story or anecdote, usually with a suggestion of smut, and well designed to put his audience in a good humor, and at the appropriate moment he moved in for the kill with his nostrum. The term "kill" may be interpreted literally, in view of the usual content of the cure-alls sold.

More sophisticated medicine men, in pursuit of higher takes, operated from cariages or vehicles of some kind, each flanked by two torch lights, with an attendant in uniform to deliver the medicine and collect the cash. Some of them maintained a black-faced artist strumming a banjo and singing Negro songs to attract and hold a crowd large enough to justify the oratory which preceded the vending of the cure-all. One example of this sophisticated school had for a stooge a real live Indian, with complete regalia of feathers and war paint. This aborigine made a short speech in his native dialect—since no one could comprehend what was said, if anything, it was all the more impressive and placed the halo of authenticity on the Indian remedy offered.

. One religious fanatic I remember as appearing in this plaza delivered about the nuttiest harangue on record. His entire diatribe was directed against wealth in all its forms: a rich man, he said, was predestined to be shunted to the lower regions, his wealth was trash and probably stolen at that! He wound up his oration, of which I have merely recorded a high spot by saying "Jesus Christ told me to throw my money away,"—whereupon he reached into his coat pocket, came out with a handful of chicken feed—nickles, dimes, quarters and half-dollars—and threw it into the crowd. This prophet was wise: if passing the hat will disperse a crowd, throwing money at them will have the opposite effect! I do not know how he accomplished his final pitch, though I am sure he did. At the expense of two smashed fingers, I snared one dollar and sixty five cents and went away from there. My conscience must have been dormant, even then: certainly it never condemned me for the possession of such vast and unearned wealth.

The scissors-grinder was a regular feature of entertainment on our local landscape. His grinding apparatus was mounted on two wheels and shoved ahead like a hand truck. Ringing a bell and crying out "scissors to grind" was his method of announcing his presence. The gadget he pushed consisted of a small grind-stone, turned by a foot pedal, with a can of water over the stone that delivered a drop at a time to cool the stone. Also in this category was the umbrella mender. He carried, swung over his shoulder, something resembling a modern golf bag, but much larger, which held cloth and ribs for umbrellas. A small tool kit carried in one hand completed his outfit. Both of these gentlemen dispensed anecdotes and gossip along with their services.

The coal peddler was a daily sight in the poorer quarters of the West End. Many occupants of tenements and upstairs apartments had no adequate storage space for coal and, if they did have it, would probably have been unable to buy the article by the load. The coal peddler had a one-horse wagon with a crude wooden box at the rear. This was attached to a steelyard and into it he shoveled the coal, usually sixty pounds or one bushel at a time. Smaller lots were sold by the bucket, at five cents each.

The vendor of wooden blocks, suitable for chopping into kindling, was in evidence in the late summer and early fall, when the more opulent of the householders were prepared to pay cash for a winter's supply of this essential commodity. A small one-horse wagonload of these blocks sold for one dollar to one dollar and twenty-five cents. Selling this way encouraged commerce, for it produced a chore for someone to reduce these blocks to sticks suitable for starting fires. For this chore the small boy of the family was generally enlisted and, with diligence, he could sometimes collect the large sum of one dollar for an eight hour job. The entire load was reduced to sticks and then stacked in some conveinent spot for use during the winter. There was little central heating then and fires had to be renewed daily, requiring an ample supply of kindling.

Rags and old iron were collected all the year round by the ragman. He had a musical call that he chanted as his spavined horse ambled slowly along the street, providing another source of free entertainment. Householders saved their rags meticulously, as a bagful brought about fifteen cents and scrap iron a half cent per pound—a good price providing the buyer's scales were kosher. This offal was quite a source of income for the small fry who often went far afield to the wholesale section of the city in the bottoms to explore barrels of trash standing in alleys awaiting removal. All sorts of treasures dear to the juvenile heart could be found in this district; long pieces of tough twine, suitable for plaiting whip crackers, scraps of leather for sling shots, and a multiplicity of junk we had no immediate use for but thought we might have at some future time. Any kind of metal was a source of wealth and would be hoarded until a sufficient quantity was on hand to interest the buyer of old iron.

Hucksters—also distinguished by their peculiar chants—with wagonloads of potatoes, apples, and other staples paraded the poorer sections and in season offered watermelons, muskmelons (to-day's aristocratic canteloupe), and any other produce they could buy at a low price from the commission house when there was a surplus.

Street stands were located at strategic corners vending bananas, popcorn, oranges, peanuts, etc. In addition to such open stands, others of a more elaborate kind were placed against the blank wall of a house and constructed so they could be closed up at night. Such stands carried fruit and candies in considerable variety and were really stores on a small scale. Riddles were a favorite amusement and one current at the time is worth recording. "Why is a banana stand like the setting sun?" Answer, "because the dago's with it." Italians were dagos, Negroes were niggers, Germans were dutch, and the Irish, micks. This did not seem to handicap any of them particularly.

Throughout the most recent fifty or sixty year period of his career William C. Smith has tended toward the conservative in dress: soft brown hat, dark—preferably brown—suit, worn without waistcoat but with a well-starched expanse of white shirt, set off with gold cuff links and a heavy gold watch chain and, invariably, a bow tie. Undoubtedly he must own four-in-hand cravats (acquired by gift, though certainly not by purchase) but he has never permitted himself to be seen in public wearing one of them.

His charming wife has, a time or two, persuaded him to have tailored something gaudier in the way of suiting—perhaps a very dark Oxford gray: once fitted and delivered he almost never wears these.

But in his early prime—says the years 1885-1895, he either wore or carefully observed the flashier raiment of his contemporaries: otherwise he could not describe it in such careful detail.

10
Sartorial Scenery

The male animal of the Eighties was a slave to the customs of his time. Certain types of clothing and adornment, including whiskers, were mandatory. His outer covering was strictly limited as to time and place. For every-day wear there was requisite a sack-coat, a vest, and trousers. The sack-coat was usually of the style in vogue to-day but was cut away to a greater degree and appeared small in comparison to the modern article. These three garments were all tailored from the same pattern of cloth, except in the case of the ultra stylish who affected a coat and vest of plain cloth in conjunction with striped pants. Pants were lined with light cotton material and the bottom stiffened by the insertion of a sheet of rubber between the cloth and the lining. A hot iron was then run over the cloth and the bottoms of the trousers were frozen into shape.

For Sunday wear, either the Prince Albert or the cutaway was the style of the more opulent citizens or at least the more hopeful. The Prince Albert was much like the modern type but the straight lines of to-day were then bell-shaped; flaring out at the hips. The cutaway, sometimes called the "swallow-tail," was usually constructed of figured cloth, cut away sharply in front with two tails behind.

The pockets in the side of the coat were false but a flap was sewed on to give the similitude of pockets. *Real* pockets would have marred the streamlining; however, there was a pocket in each tail where a kerchief and other impedimenta could be stored.

Fancy vests, usually of the double-breasted breed, came in figured material and a variety of colors. Plain white vests which could be laundered were affected by opulent saloon-keepers, bartenders, and gamblers. All clothing at that time came in two weights; winter and summer, the better variety was all wool or all worsted cloth; the cheaper, a mixture of cotton and wool. The poorest article was known as shoddy.

Overcoats were nearly always made in plain cloth with an occasional tweed. They were not as ample in cut as the modern type, were always lined, and were usually adorned with velvet collars.

A *gentleman* could wear only two types of hat: he had his choice of a "plug" or a derby. The "plug," also termed the silk-hat or the top-hat, had an elevation of some twelve inches above the brim, sometimes with straight lines, at other times flared to the top. Some were made of plain cloth, usually silk. The derby was in use by business men, clerks, and the rest of the white collar tribe.

The soft hat, known as the "slouch" was for bums and school boys. The latter also wore a flat hat about three inches high above the brim, folded in at the top. Flat straw hats of the stiff-brimmed variety were the vogue for summer wear and were decorated with gaudy bands. For the small fry, some genius invented a hat that would fit any juvenile cranium, from pin-heads to fat-heads. This triumph of ingenuity was loosely woven of cheap straw with a quarter inch ribbon for a band. Take off the ribbon and the hat could be expanded to fit an elephant or shrunk to a number six. Such hats retailed from ten to fifteen cents and, though scarcely worth the price, were both popular and expendable.

Currently constructed buildings and the shirts then in vogue had something in common; they both had iron fronts. These collarless shirts had a four inch slit cut in back with a button at the top of the slit. The insertion of this article was a difficult chore: both arms were extended toward heaven in an attitude of supplication, the extended arms were then inserted in the starched sleeves and the structure dragged down over the head. Minute embroidered holes were spotted down the center of the bosom, providing a home for the studs and these had to be inserted. A small triangular flap at the bottom of the bosom had a buttonhole designed to be attached to the top button of the trousers to keep the bosom from bulging. (That button-hole was never quite as large as the button). The separate collars then in use came in several varieties, all laundered to a throat-cutting stiffness. They were "stand-up," "lay-down," and "white-wing"; the latter with a couple of extension flares. For the *hoi polloi,* or even the elegant who might wish to make a genteel appearance and still avoid the charges of a laundry, paper collars which could be worn several days and thrown away and celluloid collars which would be washed at home or in the river were popular articles. Another attachment that no gentleman could be without were separate cuffs, starched and laundered to the stiffness of shirt bosoms. They were designed to attach to the shirt sleeves with a metal gimmick and permitted an exposure of not over three-quarters of an inch. No doubt there was a regulatory police order.

Neckties came in a number of styles. There was the bow tie, either straight or bat shaped, and it varied but little from those in use at the present time. A tie resembling the modern four-in-hand in appearance was made up in a solid piece with a strap of the same material to run under the collar. This strap had a wooden slab in the end which inserted in a slit in the tie and clinched with a pin welded into the interior. Another type was called the puff tie; this horror was invented by some architect who could have been better employed constructing outhouses. It comprised a wad of figured silk, four inches wide by six inches long with the same mechanical arrangement, strap and pin as in other ready-to-wear ties. Ready-made bow ties with a rubber loop that could be attached to the front collar button were in use by the morons who could not solve the mystery of constructing a bow. Collar buttons, front and back, came in two sizes, the front button with a long shank, a short shank in back. The front button was the heavy duty article; it was built to accommodate the shirt, two segments of collar and possibly a made-up bow tie.

The well-dressed male carried quite an assortment of impedimenta on his person. If a cigar addict, he had a leather case holding half a dozen cigars resting in the inside coat pocket and possibly a trimming instrument if his dental occlusion was bad. Cigarettes were usually left in the original package or placed in a metal box. A metal match box was essential: these came in tin, silver, or gold according to the financial rating of the smoker. A gold toothpick and a log chain which stretched across the corporation were standard equipment for the aristocracy. The toothpick was housed in a metal container two inches in length and about half the thickness of a lead pencil; a twist of the container brought forth a small triangular sliver of gold and the proud possessor of the gadget could then stand in front of a hotel around noon and display his opulence whether he had lunched at the hotel or at some quick-and-dirty. All hotels and restaurants of the better class placed a container of wooden toothpicks on each table; the ultra elite substituted goose quills, whittled to a fine point at one end.

The corporate log chain came in two sizes; one reached from the button on the vest to the left hand vest pocket where it was attached to a hunting case watch. (The open faced watch was then used only by railroad employees.) A larger chain covered the entire width of the front facade, with a watch in one pocket and a penknife attached to the other end. On the inner, or vest-button end, dangled a short length of chain terminating in a cluster of seals and charms, or a fob made of silk cloth with a monogrammed bar. Sometimes this fob dangled direct from the vest pocket. This type was made to order for pickpockets. A silver snuff box for the older generation completes the inventory.

Certainly the author had no business in saloons, even the Cincinnati family variety, in the Eighties when he was eight to eighteen years old. Be that as it may, his friends have no doubt that he not only saw those interiors in that period but was probably also well aware of what they had to offer in the way of refreshment.

His dictum on the subject may be considered authentic in the final degree:

11
The Cincinnati Saloon, 1880-90

The saloons in the West End were not as gaudy as the gilded palaces of sin located farther down town—the Mecca, Foucar's, and others. In the West End, a bar with a brass rail usually took up half of the room; a shelf backed by a mirror held a display of whiskey of various brands, gin, wine, etc. Such bottled brands were for the use of a select few, most of the patrons imbibing what was called bar whiskey. Of this there were two kinds: rye and bourbon. These were stored in barrels in the cellar, brought aloft in two or three gallon jugs, and then decanted into bottles. Such bar whiskey was cut to 85 or 90 proof. Bottles were of different shapes, one variety containing rye, the other bourbon, so that no label was needed. Scotch may have been known to more sophisticated West Enders, but to display it publicly as a beverage would have required more daring than even West End bartenders possessed. There was not a heretic among them.

A two and one half ounce glass and the bottle were placed on the bar before the patron, with a glass of water for a chaser on the side, and he helped himself. The only limit to quantity was his conscience and the size of the glass. The glass of water which flanked the whiskey was usually ignored, except by the effete. There were a few calls for whiskey and seltzer, which was in use in most places in lieu of soda, and which was also used to dilute wine. The term "highball" was unheard; it was a later invention.

Cocktails were few in variety and comparatively simple in the West End. Central Avenue saloons, like those on Vine Street north of Seventh, the beginning of the German quarter, then and later were consecrated to the sale of beer. The more sophisticated and elegant saloons in the downtown section and the bars in the hotels, served a greater variety of cocktails and knew how to concoct them. In asking a West End bartender for a mixed drink that required several ingredients and a certain amount of skill in the making, the consumer ran a grave risk. The plain sturdy bartender of our neighborhood was likely to come up with a mixture made by guess and by God, and which, when shot down the red lane to one's interior gave positive evidence that God had a very small part in the process.

Nearly all saloons displayed a sign "Wine and Beer Saloon." Why wine was given preference is a moot question, as little of it was dispensed. Maybe the word "wine" was thought by saloon-keepers to denote elegance. Certainly any saloon that had two or three bottles on hand was unusually well stocked.

Beer was delivered to the neighborhood saloons in the West End and elsewhere in kegs holding eight gallons. Such kegs were built of staves two inches thick and were bound with heavy iron straps. Some saloons mounted these kegs on a wooden horse, so called, a contraption built to accommodate one keg in a horizontal position and slanted so the keg could be drained of all it contained. The keg and its contents were not usually iced, but dispensed cellar cold as it came from the brewery. Some of the West End saloons had large refrigerators, then called "ice boxes" as the term refrigerator was not yet in use. Such ice boxes had a capacity of two kegs, each resting on a wooden horse. A large brass faucet was driven into one end of the keg with a wooden mallet and in some cases an additional dingus was inserted in the bung hole. A few of the faucets had a pump attachment which was worked by hand at intervals.

In most neighborhoods, the bucket trade was a considerable factor in the day's business; a nickel's worth of beer provided two good-sized glasses. A skilled bartender would size up the bucket offered and run the beer into it direct from the faucet; others used a measure containing about a pint to fill the customer's vessel accurately. In case the purchaser was aware of his favorite saloon-keeper's habit of running the product directly into the container, he would lard the inside of the bucket, thereby killing the foam and increasing by a worth-while margin the amount of solid beer he received for his nickel.

Neighborhood parties could, on order, purchase a small keg of beer called a pony, containing four gallons. These ponies sold for the then substantial sum of ninety cents. The term "pony" was also applied to the dispensing of whiskey. The universal price for a slug of whiskey in the West End was ten cents, but if the buyer was in low water financially, or wanted a short drink instead of a slug, the bartender was then expected to put out a small glass, with a stem like a goblet, the upper part holding something less than an ounce which the bartender dispensed with his own hand. This was probably done by way of insurance to keep the patron from surrounding the upper part of the glass with a thumb and finger and thereby securing an unauthorized amount of liquid.

On the east side of Central Avenue, between Seventh and George Streets, were located four saloons, with another on the opposite corner of Seventh. These were all beer joints with the exception of the one which adjoined our house next door on the south. This one was operated by William Hudson, an Englishman who catered to the more aristocratic inhabitants of the neighborhood. His establishment charged a higher rate than the run of the mine saloons thereabouts. I remember my grandfather complaining that Hudson charged fifteen cents for a glass of whiskey. His were largely whiskey and wine customers, who might also order a few of the simple variety of cocktails; the beer trade was beneath Hudson.

On the corner of Central Avenue and George Street was Longinotti's beer saloon. As a young but ambitious lad I had many occasions to visit Longinotti's place; not on my own account, as we had a saloon on our own premises, but as an undercover agent for a wholesale purchaser of beer. Dunholter's bakery was located on the corner of Sixth Street and Wood Alley. The store fronted on Sixth Street with the bake shop at the rear and fronting on George Street. Bakers, thirsty souls, would several times a day develop a yen for the amber fluid. It was the chore of any lucky boy who happened to be on hand at such times to be sent to Longinotti's in quest of refreshment. Frequently, through foresight, I was the lucky boy. The method of transportation, five or six buckets comprising a load, was undoubtedly the invention of some forgotten genius, who, his talents propertly directed, might have invented the telephone or toilet paper. A broomstick was utilized with nails driven part way into the wood at six inch intervals. Strung along this contraption were five or six home-made buckets. No regular buckets being available, a substitute was hatched out, consisting of fruit tins with holes drilled into the sides, into which was strung wire for handles. For this chore, or rather public service, the usual compensation was a doughnut, a cake, or a slab of zwiebach, warm, with a hole punched in the center in which was placed a lump of sugar, the whole diluted with a trickle of water. It was remarkable that these containers were usually filled solid with beer, no foam, which would indicate to a suspicious mind that the bakers either larded the buckets or had made an arrangement with the Longinotti bartender to put the foam on the bottom.

Muehe's beer saloon, in our corner store-building, was a typical beer joint with a limited stock of whiskey and wine on the side. The place measured sixteen by fifty feet, half the space taken up by the bar with the back part studded with tables. There was a side door on Seventh Street graced by a sign "Ladies Entrance." This rear part was utilized by mixed groups of people in the neighborhood for an evening's outing and also by a coterie of Germans playing pinochle.

Back of this was a lean-to of one story adjoining our Seventh Street house entrance, with two windows looking out on our yard. This was the cook house for the free lunch and also for the regular lunch served at noon, priced at fifteen cents. The amount of meat consumed daily must have run to fifty or sixty pounds. The owner's father had been imported from Germany to serve as chef of the establishment. This old gentleman became friendly with a cat I owned at the time and would often toss the animal a chunk of meat weighing up to half a pound. It spoiled the beast; the sybarite coming to prefer raw meat to the liver we normally provided. Liver, now a luxury, was then passed out as lagniappe with the purchase of other meat and was called cat meat.

There were two notable saloons, not in the West End but on Walnut Street, at the site of the Traction Building. These adjoining stores were about twelve feet in width, one of them operated by a certain Drach, the other, whose name escapes me, noted for a specialty termed "sharp beer." This came in quart bottles and was highly carbonated; being without any brewer's name on the containers it was evidently bottled on the premises. Combined with the aged sharp cheddar on the lunch counter, it was a great attraction for the homeward bound clerks and business men who kept the place crowded from five to six in the evening—until the day that something went wrong with the carbonizing equipment and blew out the entire front of the place.

All saloons provided something in the way of free lunch. In most places a simple spread of cheese, sausage, pretzels, pickles, etc., was tendered. Others, operating on a more elaborate scale, served soup and hot meat in addition to the customary layout. A hot dog—which was a good-sized bologna sausage—with two slices of rye bread and plenty of mustard, sold for five cents, with a scuttle of suds at the same price. Ham and cheese sandwiches were five cents each, and the ham was not carved with a safety razor but was thick enough to provide a job for your molars and the rye bread was of the dark variety with a distinct flavor not found in the anemic stuff now on the market. Pig's knuckles and kraut were offered in some saloons—fifteen cents for a man's sized serving and with a reasonable amount of foaming balloon juice to wash it down. This was a treat for the gods—anybody's gods.

Members of the aristocracy among bartenders were usually decorated with a couple of headlights in the shape of a glittering rock on the ring finger and another screwed into the middle of the stiff bosomed shirt in vogue at the time. Such opulence was readily accounted for; in those free and easy times there were no cash registers to safeguard the take and the bartender got his hooks on it first. How the division was made and what percentage was allotted to the owner is a moot question, but there was evidently enough to go round as all seemed to prosper. Bartenders may have operated on the system that was then current among railroad conductors. These gentry were said to toss the day's take in the air and whatever stuck to the bell cord belonged to the company; what fell on the floor was theirs and as they had to stoop to pick it up, came under the head of earned increment. Bartenders probably used the chandeliers in their joints for the same purpose.

Saturday nights, with the sidewalks crowded, the saloons on Central Avenue did a land-office business. The night trade was good on other evenings, and in most cases accounted for the bulk of the daily receipts, but Saturday night was the gala night of the week. Saturday was pay day, and after five days of economy the inhabitants had a feeling of opulence that sometimes lasted through Monday but not often.

A political parade, a circus parade, or one of the pageants that were held yearly were godsends to the saloon keeper. Patrons stood three and four deep at the bar, beer being passed over the heads of those in the front line to those in the rear. On such occasions an extra hand was employed to take care of the rush and two or more kegs of beer were on tap at the same time.

Nearly all the saloons on Central Avenue could be classed as neighborhood enterprises, depending on the trade in the immediate vicinity. There were no residences on the Avenue, only stores and saloons that occupied the ground floors of the two or three-story buildings. A few furniture stores occupied entire buildings but these were rare exceptions. The upper two or three floors were most frequently used as living quarters, frankly called tenements. Such quarters were limited in space, with few facilities, so it is understandable that their occupants would in the evening adjourn to a nearby saloon for a little recreation and a change of atmosphere. An expenditure of fifteen or twenty cents was sufficient to provide an evening's entertainment as a large percentage of the population were Germans who had a habit of lingering a long time over a glass of beer, whereas Americans tossed it down and yelled for a refill.

Such places as had a side entrance maintained what was called a sitting room. It was sometimes in the rear end of the saloon but more often a separate room that insured some degree of privacy. Such places were patronized by the women in the neighborhood, singly and in groups, oftener with a male escort. Sitting rooms were operated in an orderly manner: you could take your wife or best girl for a libation without fear of molestation by any of the less couth habitués.

The lower class joints utilized their sitting rooms for a more ulterior purpose. They were the hang-out of what were termed "sitters," a name applied to those females who practised the oldest profession in the world, had no regular habitat, but preferred sitting to walking. Such disreputable establishments used the entire building, the upper floors furnished as bedrooms affording accommodations for the "sitters" and such of the male species as succumbed to their charms.

The Sunday closing law was in force at the time I am recalling and a saloon that was fortunate enough to be located on a corner or had a side entrance leading to the upper floors was in luck. The lights were dim, the curtains down, but with the side door open the beer flowed freely. Others not endowed with such facilities stationed a guard at the front door whose duty it was to keep an eye open for the police and, when they were not in evidence, to admit patrons. On the whole the police paid little attention to such violations of the law, and guards were only essential in cases where the saloon-keeper and the man on the beat were not on good terms. Any time of the day it was a common sight to see the bartender slip into the back room with a glass of hops intended for the policeman in waiting. Free beer was one of the perquisites of a policeman's job and fortunate was he whose beat provided a number of havens where beer and lunch could be had without purse or scrip.

Nearly all the saloons at that time had their floors covered with sawdust and as tobacco chewing was an almost universal habit, gaboons were placed at strategic intervals for the chewers' use.

But most masticators of the weed were either nearsighted, blind, or just didn't give a damn; they shot the juice in the general direction of the gaboons but seldom hit the target. No matter, there was plenty floor space to take up the slack and the moisture was a factor in keeping down the dust when the porter swept out the joint sometime after midnight.

Psychologists claim that sensations recorded by the olfactory nerves are more potent and will linger in the memory long after other sensations have faded. In viewing the bar-rooms of to-day, with their vast array of glassware, numerous bottles of whiskey, gin and cordials, with ornate leather topped stools where one can rest in comfort instead of standing on one hind leg while pawing for the foot rail with the other one, there is only a difference of degree. The decor is the same but on a varying elaborate scale. However, the oldster has a vague sense of something missing, something lacking in the picture. It's the odor of the old time saloon created by a combination of fresh sawdust and stale beer. It would rise up and smite you the moment you entered the place. It was a homely smell and in time one became accustomed to it as one would be content with hanging if the process was sufficiently prolonged to become familiar.

The odor produced by a mixture of stale beer and sawdust was a by-product of the froth-blower's union, an organization with a ritual that consisted of blowing the foam off the top of the glass onto the floor; this custom was almost universal. The anarchists of that period believed in direct action and considered wading through two inches of foam an extra-curricular activity that paid no dividends.

Bottled beer was served on demand in most saloons and was also delivered to the consumer by the breweries. A case of so-called pints (twelve ounces) comprised twelve bottles and was delivered for home consumption at the rate of forty-five or fifty cents per case; cases of larger bottles containing twenty-five ounces came at around ninety cents.

"Schooner houses," as they were known "Over the Rhine" in the German quarter of the city, had no place in the West End. A schooner was a tall glass with a flared top, about ten inches high and four inches across the top, the bottom running to a point. This vessel, designed to create the impression of quantity, was a delusion as the foam was in residence in the upper part while the beer lived below. Net content probably was no more and perhaps less than was served in the standard glass with a handle on the side, which held from eight to ten ounces.

Bock beer was a popular drink in the spring of the year. This was beer brewed from charred grain and was much darker in color than the standard lager. This beverage was announced by colorful signs depicting a goat (German "Bock") with a long beard, holding a large container of the elixir with his front foot. This brew was limited in quantity and only obtainable for a few weeks in the spring. One genius in our vicinity, evidently a disciple of Plato, demonstrated the existence of Plato's universals by having the brewery reserve a number of kegs of the Bock which he dispensed on July fourth.

On Sixth Street between Central Avenue and Plum were located two saloons that were not saloons in our accepted sense of the term: in Old English they would have been called "boozing kens." We knew them as "barrel houses" and their stock in trade was limited to whiskey, gin, and other hard liquors. Instead of the plain fronts of regular saloons, they had show windows in which were displayed bottles of whiskey of various sizes ranging from a half-pint to a quart. These were decorated with gaudy labels and priced as low as fifteen cents for a half pint to one dollar for a quart of aged whiskey. Some of these were compounds that were termed—with no excuse whatever—"rectified whiskey." Such compounds often consisted of alcohol, distilled water, burnt sugar for coloring, bead oil, and rye or bourbon flavoring. In rare cases in which the compounder was squeamish or even honest, a modicum of good whiskey was added, assisted by a little glycerine or castor oil to take the scratch out of the alcohol. *Blended whiskey,* a mixture of two or more brands of different age or vintage, was preferred by some addicts. Some of these blends were nationally known and often provided a smoother drink than the straight article. In my opinion, so-called modern "blends" are nothing but the old "rectified" compounds masking under an alias: I, personally, wouldn't take a slug of modern blend if I was dying of snakebite.

{*He would too!*—FLAXIUS, *ed.*}

One wall of the interior of the typical barrel house was fitted up with shelves carrying a stock of the various brands displayed in the show window; the other side of the room was lined with fifty-gallon barrels of whiskey, placed on the floor in racks with a second tier on the top of the first. Each barrel had a spigot from which was drawn the supply as needed for bulk sales to customers who purchased some special brand by the quart or gallon. Across the rear was a primitive bar some inches higher than the regular saloon bar, consisting of a plain varnished board about ten feet long by eighteen inches wide. Back of this bar on one side was a barrel of whiskey standing on end with a spigot in the lower part from which the liquid was dispensed directly from the barrel to the customer's glass.

On a shelf next to the wall various brands of liquor were in evidence, some labeled and others in plain bottles, the quality of the latter known only to God and the proprietor. These emporiums were patronized by the Irish and American inhabitants who believed their stomachs to be lined with a substance that beer might corrode, whereas whiskey apparently acted only as a preservative and polishing agent.

A credit system was in operation in most saloons in a limited way: any of the regular patrons known to be reliable could, at the tail-end of the week when funds were low, get their regular libations and have it "put on the slate" until Saturday. This system was the father of the shortest conversation, using the greatest economy of words, recorded in barroom history. A new bartender in one of the saloons on Central Avenue, an Irishman named Mike, served a chap named Casey a drink of whiskey. Casey promptly swallowed the slug and then told Mike to put it on the slate. Mike, in doubt as to Casey's standing, went over to the dumb waiter and called the proprietor, who resided on the upper floor, for a credit rating and the following conversation is said to have taken place:

Mike: "Is Casey good for a drink?"
Boss: "Has he it?"
Mike: "He has."
Boss: "He is."

Inasmuch as Casey buried the slug where the cat couldn't get it, there was nothing the proprietor could do but endorse the transaction.

Sanitary safeguards were few and primitive but as germs had not yet been invented and all diseases were considered acts of God, there was probably little need for them.

A couple or three steel forks were all the implements in sight on the lunch counter. They were common forks—that is, they were used in common by such patrons as were too effete to use their fingers. There was no need for knives—the lunch was prefabricated and cut to size. Beer and whiskey glasses, after use, were simply rinsed in cold water and if there was a rush on, no attempt was made to dry them. A few of the saloons kept a couple of towels held in a metal clip dangling from the front of the bar for the use of their more particular customers. One dissenter on Central Avenue, the only heretic in the neighborhood, spread white sand on his saloon floor in place of sawdust. Possibly it was some latent artistic instinct in his make-up that inspired this measure; certainly the contrast between the rich russet color of tobacco juice was more aesthetic when spotted on contrasting white than it was when sprayed on roughly harmonizing sawdust. I wish I could recall that saloon-keeper's name: possibly it was Reubens—he must have had some heritage of genius.

Beer had a utilitarian value not known to the cognoscenti of today: used as a substitute for water it made an excellent whitewash. The price asked for whitewashing the walls in our back yard by one of the colored brethren was two dollars—in competition, not being a member of the union, I took the job for one dollar, out of which I had to provide the lime, which cost ten cents. Our saloon keeper tenant, co-operating in my effort to maintain free enterprise, agreed to assist me and saved a couple of gallons of stale beer salvaged from the drip can under the faucet in his draft keg. I mixed this with the water and lime, achieved a handsome effect and the net profit, ninety cents, went a long way in the purchase of contraband commodities. This gain was probably utilized as the initial deposit of a hoard I was developing for the purchase of some much-wanted article that ran to several dollars in cost. Such plans usually came to naught: saving over a long period was a difficult chore—usually I would acquire almost enough to pay for what I had in mind when Satan would tempt me to indulge in some minor luxury that played havoc with my good intentions.

A few saloons used a back room for gambling, where poker and craps were the order of the day. Some games were backed by the house, while others were operated by local groups paying the proprietor a fixed charge or setting up a "kitty" to compensate the owner. Dice were used at most bars in shaking for the drinks, the old game of horse and horse. This was gravy for the owner. If he lost, he paid off in drinks that cost but half the amount of the wager; if he won he collected cash for drinks he did not imbibe.

"Them days are gone forever." The old saloon with its friendly owners, and the bartenders who were the official repository for the trials and troubles of their customers, have been replaced by glittering glassware, chromium fixings and bartenders with all the dignity of an Archbishop in whom no one, unless in an advanced state of intoxication, would dare to confide his troubles. The old personal touch has vanished; the old "home away from home" is no more.

We can still drown our troubles in the modern bistro but we have to immerse them without benefit of clergy. Some day, before I am relegated to the realm of eternal bliss, I am going to buy a plug of tobacco (if I can find such an article in these degenerate times) fit up a box with sawdust and indulge in one last chaw: but first I shall pour a foaming glass of beer and blow a little suds on that sawdust—just for old time's sake.

Tailpiece

The descendant of Simon Legree who prodded me into writing these memoirs of the last Century, tells me I have constructed an incomplete dog; a dog with an essential element omitted, namely, the tail. I admit that such a dog is lacking in symmetry and that some sort of caudal appendage is in order by way of comparison of the old days with the present rat race.

This leaves me with a choice between the frying pan and the fire.

If I put in a plug for the old days, I will be crucified by the present generation of jazz fiends, rock-and-roll idiots, movie addicts and television nitwits—whose name is legion. *But* there would be none to join and support me on the defense side, as most of my contemporaries are either dead or senile. If I plead for the present time, I will be accused of political chicanery, lying for votes, catering to the majority who, as a noted French diplomat said "are always wrong."

So I shall appear in court with a list of "agreed statement of facts," and let the jury decide.

During the last quarter of the past century, life went on at a leisurely pace. Social intercourse, except among the elite, was casual and unarranged in advance. Evenings were spent in conversation including the latest scandal, politics, current events, the contemporary production of the pens of currently popular novelists, the Civil War and, in the higher intellectual brackets, the impact of the Darwinian theory on current theology, Spencer's philosophy and the hilarious debate between Huxley and Gladstone about what were generally referred to, locally, as "the Gaberdine Swine."

During the Eighties and Nineties Cincinnati had some half dozen theatres, all of them running the full season with weekly shows. There was naturally some scandal about members of the theatrical profession but as most practitioners stuck to their wenches until Father Time released them from bondage there was little for the public to hash over.

Diseases, such as typhoid, scarlet fever and small pox were rampant; it was a common sight to see a house plastered with a red or yellow poster, indicating that the premises were quarantined. The span of life was shorter than the present expectancy—but there were fewer deaths from heart failure in the forty-five to sixty bracket. Sanitation was primitive, germs had not been invented and medical science was largely in the experimental stage. Such matters are better controlled today.

As to the comparative cost of living, this is a moot question; in an argument I had with a local economist, some years ago, he claimed that in view of the difference in wages and income, one could live much better today than in the last century. He had some figures to prove this. I don't know—but in those days a six room house could be had for two thousand dollars, and furnished for two hundred. Today, in addition to the price of a home, one must have an automobile, television, radio, washing machine, electric sweeper and a number of other life saving gadgets all of which must come out of income after the initial bite that Uncle Sam and some states put on one's take, plus sales tax and a few hundred other taxes wrapped up in anything one buys. The aforesaid economist waived this aside as having no bearing on the question, but as Bill Nye once said, "facts are stubborn things." We mortgage our home to buy a car, we put a plaster on the car to build a garage and mortgage the garage to buy gasoline which will enable us to visit night clubs and hot spots where beer is no longer five cents a glass and the free lunch is absorbed in a two dollar minimum.

Cincinnati today lists over seventy five so-called "loan and finance companies," some of them with half a dozen branches. All occupy high-priced locations and all seem to flourish. Even the leading banks have invaded the profitable chattel mortgage field which, in the old days, was tilled by a few loan sharks and the pawn shops.

These things seem to me to add up to the chief differences between then and now. Were the old days best? You take the question: I pass.

www.ingramcontent.com/pod-product-compliance
Lightning Source LLC
Chambersburg PA
CBHW030351100526
44592CB00010B/915